Character:
The Foundation of Leadership

Six Week Daily Devotional

Robert L. Vernon

Character: The Foundation of Leadership Six Week Daily Devotional
By Robert L. Vernon
June 2009
© Copyright RLV 2005

ISBN: 0-9824379-1-9
ISBN-13: 978-0-9824379-1-9
Published by Pointman Leadership Institute, Monument, CO

Robert L. Vernon
P.O. Box 392
Bonsall, California 92003
United States of America

Introduction

This book is designed to be a guide for six weeks of daily devotions. A portion of the Bible is presented for each daily reading. Comments and questions are included to generate thought and application of the principles presented.

Everyone should be interested in leadership, men and women alike. True leadership means being the type of influence in others' lives that causes them to choose to follow your guidance as an act of their free will. If you want to influence one person, or one thousand, then this study is for you.

The Bible has much to say about leadership. It contains proverbs, quotes and stories that illustrate time tested principles that result in powerful leadership. Some of these principles are obvious and easy to understand. Others are more subtle and require much thought and analysis. In either case, they are valuable and should be sought like a treasure. When applied, these principles not only result in powerful leadership, they have utility in a more meaningful and fulfilled life. The process of diligently going through this six week devotional process has life changing potential.

This process of daily devotions will be optimized if used in conjunction with the companion book **Character: The Foundation of Leadership Small Group Discussion** (Pointman Leadership Institute, 2009). The genesis of these two books began after the development of a seminar presented to governmental leaders in over thirty countries by The Pointman Leadership Institute. Inquires can be made at www.pliglobal.com.

Tips for Using This Book

HERE IS A PREVIEW OF THE FORMAT USED IN THIS BOOK TO ENCOURAGE YOU IN YOUR DAILY BIBLE STUDY.

OBSERVE: This section is a passage (or passages) from the Bible to read and consider.

KEY PRINCIPLE: This is a brief statement to focus attention on a principle contained in the scripture passage from the previous paragraph.

UNDERSTAND: This section provides an in-depth discussion of why the key principle is important to you as a leader.

DIG DEEPER: This section contains parallel passages from the Bible that address the principle for the day.

APPLY: This section is intended to encourage the participant to apply the principle for the day to his or her own life.

PRAY: This is a suggested prayer to encourage the participant to ask God for His help in making the application to their life.

Unless otherwise indicated, all biblical references are taken from the New American Standard Bible (NASB).

Day 1

WHAT IS A "SERVANT/LEADER"?

". . . whoever wishes to become great among you shall be your servant."
Matthew 20:26

OBSERVE
Matthew 20:20–28

> *"Then the mother of the sons of Zebedee came to Him with her sons, bowing down, and making a request of Him. And He said to her, "What do you wish?" She said to Him, "Command that in Your kingdom these two sons of mine may sit, one on Your right and one on Your left." But Jesus answered and said, "You do not know what you are asking for. Are you able to drink the cup that I am about to drink?" They said to Him, "We are able." He said to them, "My cup you shall drink; but to sit on My right and on My left, this is not mine to give, but it is for those for whom it has been prepared by My Father." And hearing this, the ten became indignant with the two brothers."*

> *"But Jesus called them to Himself, and said, "You know that the rulers of the Gentiles lord it over them, and their great men exercise authority over them. It is not so among you, but whoever wishes to become great among you shall be your servant, and whoever wishes to be first among you shall be your slave; just as the Son of Man did not come to be served, but to serve, and to give His life as a ransom for many."*

KEY PRINCIPLE: True leadership means serving.

UNDERSTAND

During the last decade the concept of the "Servant/Leader" has been rediscovered. Many contemporary books about leadership are discussing this model of leadership. Some authors even use the word *"servant,"* first mandated by Jesus Christ to his disciples.

Today, like during the days Jesus was here on earth, there is much misunderstanding about leadership. To many leadership means having people serve you. Leadership has been perverted to mean status symbols, a lofty title, privileges, more money and control. But Jesus clearly describes leadership with a completely different perspective. He emphasizes serving your followers.

How does one serve his/her followers? How does one become a true leader?

It is important to realize that leadership is somewhat like health. It is not something you can demand, claim, or have conferred upon you. To a great extent, a person's health is a result of eating the right foods, maintaining an exercise program, keeping appropriate sleeping patterns, and of course inheriting good genes. While we do not choose our genes, we do make choices about our living patterns. These choices reflect character traits—traits like discipline and diligence. Likewise, leadership is the result of specific character traits and the resulting actions. The attributes of a good leader, such as respect, authority, and credibility, are not things that can be conferred upon or given to an individual. They must be earned. Jesus said they must be earned by serving. But what exactly does He mean by "serving"? During this study we will probe the specifics of serving. We will discover what the Bible has to say about servant/leadership. Because it is through acts of serving that leadership emerges. This involves the "Backward Principle." To lead you must serve. In the verse from Proverbs listed below, you must give up in order to gain. In real life, giving up something does, in fact, result in gaining more.

For example, giving up discretionary time for exercise can result in gaining health, efficiency and eventually more discretionary time.

DIG DEEPER
John 13:3-7; Matthew 16:25, 26; Proverbs 11:24.

APPLY
What is my motivation for wanting to lead? Am I willing to learn how to serve in order to be an effective leader?

PRAY
"Dear Lord, teach me how I can serve those I want to influence. Make me willing to humble myself so I can lead."

Day 2

A SERVANT/LEADER PRESENTS CLEAR GOALS

"Go therefore and make disciples of all the nations. . . "
Matthew 28:19

OBSERVE
Luke 9:1–6; Matthew 28:18–20

> *"And He called the twelve together, and gave them power and authority over all the demons, and to heal diseases. And He sent them out to proclaim the kingdom of God, and to perform healing. And He said to them, 'Take nothing for your journey, neither a staff, nor a bag, nor bread, nor money; and do not even have two tunics apiece. And whatever house you enter, stay there, and take your leave from there. And as for those who do not receive you, as you go out from that city, shake off the dust from your feet as a testimony against them.' "*

> *"And Jesus came up and spoke to them, saying, 'All authority has been given to Me in heaven and on earth. Go therefore and make disciples of all the nations, baptizing them in the name of the Father and the Son and the Holy Spirit, teaching them to observe all that I commanded you; and lo, I am with you always, even to the end of the age.' "*

KEY PRINCIPLE: A servant/leader gives the followers clear goals and direction.

UNDERSTAND
Leadership is intertwined with the concept of goals. The word *"lead"* itself indicates movement. It can be actual physical movement or movement of a more conceptual and difficult nature. To lead implies that there is a direction or a choice of alternative directions in which to

move. Perhaps there is a perceived need to move from a static state to action. Or there may be a desire to move from a certain level of accomplishment to a higher one. It can involve movement from one philosophy to another or from one strategy to another. But it always involves movement of some type. People who are successful as leaders know where they are going. They have a clearly defined objective that they have a *passion* to achieve.

Leaders are motivated for some reason to convince others to achieve certain goals. Effective leaders have the ability to *conceptualize* goals and then *communicate* the goals to others in a clearly understandable way. They communicate goals in such a way that the goals seem desirable and worthwhile to pursue. They also have the insight to distinguish between goals and strategies and/or tactics that are intended to achieve the goals.

In order to reach a goal, one must clearly understand what the goal is. Understanding a goal its purpose brings meaning and sense to actions, tactics, and strategies intended to reach the goal. Therefore a leader must (1) have the ability to clearly identify specific goals, (2) have the skills to effectively communicate the goals to others, and (3) secure the commitment of those being led to pursue the goals. Furthermore, effective leaders understand the necessity of *maintaining focus* on those goals. These three abilities and/or skills sound simple and straightforward. They are not. Each involves a strong commitment and plenty of hard work. Jesus did all three. He was goal oriented.

DIG DEEPER
Acts 20: 16; Mark 8: 34 – 38; 2 Timothy 2: 1,2

APPLY
Knowing that Jesus and the Apostle Paul gave clear goals and direction to their followers, how can this apply in my life?

PRAY

"Dear Lord, you gave me an example of servant/leadership by giving your disciples clear goals and direction. Please give me the wisdom and courage to do likewise."

Day 3

A SERVANT/LEADER LEADS BY EXAMPLE

"Brethren, join in following my example. . ."
Philippians 3:17

OBSERVE
Philippians 3:17–21; 1 Corinthians 4:14 -17

> *"Brethren, join in following my example, and observe those who walk according to the pattern you have in us. For many walk, of whom I often told you, and now tell you even weeping, that they are enemies of the cross of Christ, whose end is destruction, whose god is their appetite, and whose glory is in their shame, who set their minds on earthly things. For our citizenship is in heaven, from which also we eagerly wait for a Savior, the Lord Jesus Christ; who will transform the body of our humble state into conformity with the body of His glory, by the exertion of the power that He has even to subject all things to Himself."*

> *"I do not write these things to shame you, but to admonish you as my beloved children. For if you were to have countless tutors in Christ, yet you would not have many fathers; for in Christ Jesus I became your father through the gospel. I exhort you therefore, be imitators of me. For this reason I have sent to you Timothy, who is my beloved and faithful child in the Lord, and he will remind you of my ways which are in Christ, just as I teach everywhere in every church."*

KEY PRINCIPLE: Living an example is the most powerful way to lead.

UNDERSTAND

Two sons of a prominent and respected businessman were arrested by the police for stealing accessories from cars in the neighborhood. The police were somewhat puzzled since the boys displayed no guilt and yet the family seemed to be model citizens. During the interrogation of the boys the police asked if their father had not told them about the "wrongness" of stealing. The boys replied that their father had indeed told them that stealing was wrong; but that he boasted of cheating on his income tax returns.

Leadership involves commitment. Effective leaders exude the confidence that they are leading their followers in the right direction. By demonstrating confidence, the leader gives assurance to those being led that they are moving in the right direction and their goal is achievable. A very powerful way to demonstrate this confidence is to model the desired action. In other words, lead by example. *Leading by example is the most powerful way to lead.*

Confidence does not just happen. Confidence is the result of doing one's homework. People who have a confident opinion about a particular subject or issue are usually well aware of facts and data about the issue. Often they have researched the issue thoroughly. Their confidence is based upon a factual analysis and/or well-developed reason. By then taking the action he or she is asking others to do, a leader demonstrates the confidence that the action is worthwhile, possible to accomplish, and a good course of action.

> *"The first great gift we can bestow on others is a good example."*
> Thomas Morell

DIG DEEPER
John 13:15; 1 Thessalonians 1:6,7; Titus 2:7

APPLY

What do I need to begin doing (or cease from doing) so that I will be a better example to those I desire to influence?

PRAY

"Lord, please help me to be more consistent in acting out what I believe."

Day 4

A SERVANT/LEADER CONVINCES PEOPLE TO FOLLOW WILLINGLY

"And they immediately left the nets, and followed Him."
Matthew 4:20

OBSERVE
Matthew 4:18-22

> *"And walking by the Sea of Galilee, He saw two brothers, Simon who was called Peter, and Andrew his brother, casting a net into the sea; for they were fisherman. And He said to them, 'Follow me and I will make you fishers of men.' And they immediately left the nets and followed him. And going on from there He saw two other brothers, James the son of Zebedee, and John his brother, in the boat with Zebedee their father, mending their nets; and He called them. And they immediately left the boat and their father, and followed Him."*

KEY PRINCIPLE: A true leader convinces people to choose to follow as an act of free will.

UNDERSTAND
Leadership continues to influence the life and behavior of the follower(s) even outside the presence of the leader. True leadership is convincing. Rather than following out of fear of discipline or hope for reward, followers voluntarily choose to follow willingly. This is a very persuasive reason to pursue the art of leadership rather than management relying solely on rewards, sanctions and control systems.

This is one of the dimensions that contrasts leadership with management. Leadership involves salesmanship. Not an insincere "snow job" to manipulate people, but a personal conviction that translates into persuasion and influence. True leadership means that those being led follow *because they want to.* Something powerful has happened. The leader has provided a combination of credibility, information, training, logic, challenge, hope—something that has caused those being led to follow as an act of their own will. They perform the desired action, cease doing something when reproved, or strive to achieve the goal because they have "bought into it." This form of positive influence is the opposite of autocratic control often associated with management that resorts to mandates, pressure, intimidation, and force.

The disciples (followers) of Jesus Christ continued to follow His teaching after He had left the world scene. He had changed their lives forever. They were convinced that He was who He said He was. They were convinced that He spoke and lived truth. They were willing to die, rather than turn from doing His will. Most of them did just that. Jesus Christ is the greatest of all leaders. He modeled to us what leadership really means.

> *"It's not called the 'art of persuasion' for nothing.*
> *This intangible, often elusive, skill was a mainstay*
> *in Abraham Lincoln's interaction arsenal."*
> *Donald Phillips*

DIG DEEPER
Proverbs 18:19; Colossians 3:21; 2 Timothy 3:14

APPLY
What can I do to better understand why Jesus Christ was so persuasive and influential? How can I begin to be more like Him?

PRAY

"Lord, I want people to follow me as I follow you. Please help me to understand what I must do to be more like Jesus."

Day 5

A SERVANT/LEADER HAS THE DESIRE AND ABILITY TO HELP HIS OR HER FOLLOWERS DEVELOP AND PURSUE EXCELLENCE

"But now I come to Thee; and these things I speak in the world, that they may have My joy made full in themselves." John 17:13

OBSERVE
John 17:6-13

> *"I have manifested Your name to the men whom You gave Me out of the world; they were Yours and You gave them to Me, and they have kept Your word. Now they have come to know that everything You have given Me is from You; for the words which You gave Me I have given to them; and they received them and truly understood that I came forth from You, and they believed that You sent Me. I ask on their behalf; I do not ask on behalf of the world, but of those whom You have given Me; for they are Yours; and all things that are Mine are Yours, and Yours are Mine; and I have been glorified in them. I am no longer in the world; and yet they themselves are in the world, and I come to You Holy Father, keep them in Your name, the name which You have given Me, that they may be one even as We are. While I was with them, I was keeping them in Your name which You have given Me; and I guarded them and not one of them perished but the son of perdition, so that the Scripture would be fulfilled. But now I come to You; and these things I speak in the world so that they may have My joy made full in themselves."*

John 13:1

> *"Now before the Feast of the Passover, Jesus knowing that His hour had come that He should depart out of this world to the Father, having loved His own who were in the world, He loved them to the end."*

KEY PRINCIPLE: Servant/Leadership means sincerely caring about the welfare and development of the followers.

UNDERSTAND

In John 17, Jesus prays for His disciples. In that prayer one sees the deep love and concern He has for His followers. A Servant/Leader cares sincerely about the welfare of the followers. For example, this kind of leadership involves helping the followers prepare for and complete their tasks well. In this kind of leadership, the leader does not see the individuals that he or she is trying to lead as a means to an end, but rather as a major part of the end. A Servant/Leader sees those being led as fellow human beings that have similar dreams, aspirations, and needs. This kind of leadership knows that the achievement of excellence brings fulfillment and joy. Also, he/she understands that this fulfillment generates a cycle leading to higher levels of accomplishment and excellence.

From a practical standpoint, a person cannot be led to perform an act that he or she is incapable of doing. Leadership therefore includes preparing people to perform the tasks that are necessary to reach the goal. It involves equipping them with the training, skills, tools, technology, and other resources they will need to be successful. It also involves removing or minimizing barriers to goal achievement.

Someone has said that followers don't care so much about how much the leader knows; but rather how much the leader cares. It is amazing how followers will be willing to tolerate and forgive the leader for inadequacies if they know the leader sincerely cares for them.

Regular acts of interest, kindness, assistance, guidance and protection go a long way in building a willingness to follow.

DIG DEEPER
John 14:26; 2 Timothy 1:1-4; Philemon

APPLY
How can I develop a sincere caring attitude for those I desire to influence? How can I demonstrate that care to them?

PRAY
"Lord, give me the capacity to care for those I am trying to lead. Guide me to practical actions that will demonstrate that care."

Day 6

A Servant/Leader inspires followers to achieve their full potential

"But I do not consider my life of any account as dear to myself, in order that I may finish my course, and the ministry which I received from the Lord Jesus."
Acts 20:24

OBSERVE
Luke 15:26-33

> *"If anyone comes to Me, and does not hate his own father and mother and wife and children and brothers and sisters, yes, and even his own life, he cannot be My disciple. Whoever does not carry his own cross, and come after Me cannot be My disciple. For which one of you, when he wants to build a tower, does not first sit down and calculate the cost, to see if he has enough to complete it? Otherwise, when he has laid a foundation, and is not able to finish, all who observe it begin to ridicule him, saying, 'This man began to build and was not able to finish.' Or what king, when he sets out to meet another king in battle, will not first sit down and take counsel whether he is strong enough with ten thousand men to encounter the one coming against him with twenty thousand? Or else, while the other is still far away, he sends a delegation and asks terms of peace. So therefore, no one of you can be My disciple who does not give up all his own possessions."*

Acts 20:22-24

> *"And now, behold, bound in spirit, I am on my way to Jerusalem, not knowing what will happen to me there, except*

that the Holy Spirit solemnly testifies to me in every city, saying that bonds and afflictions await me. But I do not consider my life of any account as dear to myself, in order that I may finish my course, and the ministry which I received from the Lord Jesus, to testify solemnly of the gospel of the grace of God."

KEY PRINCIPLE: A Servant/Leader inspires people to follow sacrificially.

UNDERSTAND

Jesus called upon His disciples to be willing to give up everything in order to follow Him. Although initially succumbing to human frailties, they eventually endured jail, physical punishment, rejection and even death. Jesus inspired his disciples to follow sacrificially. The Apostle Paul sums up the attitude most of them must have had in Acts 20:22-24. His paramount goal was to finish the assignment that Jesus gave him.

Inspiration is more powerful than *motivation*. Motivation works when the boss is watching or there is a good chance he or she will become aware of the follower's behavior. Motivation is external and usually involves a reward and/or a sanction.

Inspiration involves touching the very core beliefs of a person. Inspiration penetrates through the intellect to the emotions. Inspiration touches a person's attitudes. The follower becomes impassioned about something upon which they place high value. Therefore effective leaders emphasize principle and matters of conviction.

To be able to inspire others, leaders must themselves be inspired. They must have a high level of sincerity and excitement about the mission. Many executives and supervisors can motivate people, but few can inspire them. People have almost unlimited potential when they are inspired, especially when working together as a team. Good leaders know that and work diligently to lift up the standard to a high level. They challenge people to reach for that high standard and somehow are able to instill in them the belief that they can reach it. Their confidence, enthusiasm, and total commitment are obvious, and therefore they are contagious.

The ability to inspire people is directly related to one's character. Leaders of strong character who demonstrate the "fruits of the Spirit", like love, joy, peace and longsuffering have the foundation necessary for inspiring others. In the passage below from the first epistle of John, he encourages us to inspire others by demonstrating care for those being led. He even uses the extreme example of being willing to lay down our lives, like Jesus--the ultimate leader--did.

> *"A gifted leader is one who is able to touch your heart"*
> J.S. Potofsky

DIG DEEPER
2 Samuel 5:1-12; Galatians 5:22-26; 1 John 3:16-23

APPLY
What practical steps can I take to allow God to inspire me to a level of commitment so that I can inspire others?

PRAY
"Lord, develop in me a level of commitment to you and your principles so profound that I can inspire others."

Day 7

DOERS OF THE WORD

"But prove yourselves doers of the word, and not merely hearers who delude themselves. For if anyone is a hearer of the word and not a doer, he is like a man who looks at his natural face in a mirror; for once he has looked at himself and gone away, he has immediately forgotten what kind of person he was. But one who looks intently at the perfect law, the law of liberty, and abides by it, not having become a forgetful hearer but an effectual doer, this man shall be blessed in what he does."
James 1:22-25

Looking back over the week, I learned . . .

Day 1 - Leadership involves serving.

Day 2 - Servant/Leaders present clear goals.

Day 3 - Servant/Leaders lead by example.

Day 4 - Servant/Leaders convince people to follow willingly.

Day 5 - Servant/Leaders care about the development and welfare of their followers.

Day 6 - Servant/Leaders inspire their followers to sacrificial commitment.

Journal Space

Lord, I am grateful for you teaching me the following:

Lord, I plan on being a leader who follows God by:

I have questions about:

Day 8

LEADERSHIP INVOLVES CHARACTER

"For the overseer must be above reproach as God's steward"
Titus 1:7

OBSERVE
Titus 1:5-9

> *"For this reason I left you in Crete, that you might set in order what remains, and appoint elders in every city as I directed you, namely, if any man be above reproach, the husband of one wife, having children who believe, not accused of dissipation or rebellion. For the overseer must be above reproach as God's steward, not self-willed, not quick-tempered, not addicted to wine, not pugnacious, not fond of sordid gain, but hospitable, loving what is good, sensible, just, devout, self-controlled, holding fast the faithful word which is in accordance with the teaching, that he may be able both to exhort in sound doctrine and to refute those who contradict."*

KEY PRINCIPLE: Good character is a requirement for leaders.

UNDERSTAND
The requirements for leadership in the Bible place a strong emphasis on good character. The phrase "beyond reproach" is used to summarize the several qualifications that are listed for an "overseer" or leader. The list of specific qualifications includes references to sexual purity, self discipline, selflessness, interested in others and a proven leader in the home.

Contemporary literature on leadership also emphasizes the importance of good character traits. Most Americans indicate Abraham Lincoln was one of the best leaders in the history of the

United States. Donald Phillips in his book, "Lincoln on Leadership," describes character as an essential element in Lincoln's success as a leader. Character is often described as a "threshold issue" in leadership. In other words, a deficit in character can cancel or reduce other leadership skills or talents.

The traditional approach in preparing people for leadership often focuses on **behavior**. There is a strong consensus on the types of behavior that lead to effective and powerful leadership. Information about effective leadership behavior has been widely disseminated during the latter part of the twentieth century. Yet at the same time there seems to be a leadership vacuum.

Our behavior is invariably linked to our core beliefs, values and ethics. Yet we have unwittingly assumed we can build a beautiful "structure" of leadership behavior without addressing the foundation of such a structure. It is appropriate and necessary to address leadership behavior; but it does not go far enough. If a building is to survive the elements, if it is to last through the stress of weather and earthquakes, then the unseen foundation is all-important. Similarly, if an observable effective leadership style is to survive, it too must be supported by a firm foundation of ethics or character. Similar to the foundation of a building, these attributes may be difficult to observe and evaluate; but they are just as important and related to behavior as a solid foundation is to a stable structure. True leadership is more related to character than a person's technical skills.

DIG DEEPER
1 Timothy 3:8-13; Proverbs 10:9; Galatians 5:22, 23

APPLY
What character traits do I need to develop in order to be a better leader?

PRAY

"Lord, help me to be humble enough to admit to myself the character traits that need improvement in my life. Show me how you can help me in this project."

Day 9

LEADERS RECOGNIZE GREAT OPPORTUNITIES AND SEIZE THE INITIATIVE

". . . for a wide door for effective service has opened to me"
1 Corinthians 16:9

OBSERVE
1 Corinthians 16:5-9

> *"But I shall come to you after I go through Macedonia, for I am going through Macedonia; and perhaps I shall stay with you, or even spend the winter, that you may send me on my way wherever I may go. For I do not wish to see you now just in passing; for I hope to remain with you for some time, if the Lord permits. But I shall remain in Ephesus until Pentecost; for a wide door for effective service has opened to me, and there are many adversaries."*

Acts 19:8-10

> *"And he entered the synagogue and continued speaking out boldly for three months, reasoning and persuading them about the kingdom of God. But when some were becoming hardened and disobedient, speaking evil of the Way before the multitude, he withdrew from them and took away the disciples, reasoning daily in the school of Tyrannus. And this took place for two years, so that all who lived in Asia heard the word of the Lord, both Jews and Greeks."*

KEY PRINCIPLE: Leaders diligently seek opportunities and seize the initiative.

UNDERSTAND

The two passages selected are related. In the letter to the Corinthians, Paul mentions an opportunity he perceives in Ephesus. In the passage from Acts, Luke records the details of how Paul boldly seized the initiative in Ephesus and chronicles the results that followed.

Many people complain that they have never had an opportunity to lead. They explain that if they only had an opportunity to do so, perhaps they could be successful. Another perspective is that true leaders diligently seek opportunities and often see them where others do not. For example, the Chinese language uses two of their characters to represent the concept of "crisis." One of the characters represents **danger,** the other character represents **opportunity**. In other words, from this perspective a "crisis" is a dangerous opportunity. No one would say they have never faced a crisis. Therefore they have probably faced a "dangerous opportunity." True leaders see problems around them as opportunities to lead.

The real question is not whether or not you will have opportunities (sometimes disguised as a crisis); but rather will you (1) recognize them as opportunities and, (2) have the courage to seize the initiative to lead. Opportunities are like windows in time that open and close. Some "windows of opportunities" are open for months, some weeks and some for only a moment in time.

During this week you will probably have several opportunities to be a positive influence in someone's life (lead). The three big questions are: (1) will you recognize the opportunity; (2) will you jump through the window before it closes; (3) will you ask God for wisdom as you seize the initiative.

DIG DEEPER

Luke 21:10-13; Colossians 4:2-5; Galatians 6:9,10

APPLY

Look diligently for opportunities this week that may appear as problems or crises. Record them on a journal page as you become aware of them. You will be surprised at how many opportunities pass your way.

PRAY

"Lord, give me the diligence to aggressively seek to perceive the opportunities that you bring my way this week. Give me the courage and wisdom to respond."

Day 10

MOTIVE IS IMPORTANT IN LEADERSHIP

". . . wait until the Lord comes who will both bring to light the things hidden in the darkness and disclose the motives of men's heart;"
1 Corinthians 4:5

OBSERVE
1 Corinthians 4:1-5

> *"Let a man regard us in this manner, as servants of Christ, and stewards of the mysteries of God. In this case, moreover it is required of stewards that one be found trustworthy. But to me it is a very small thing that I should be examined by you, or by any human court; in fact, I do not even examine myself. For I am conscious of nothing against myself, yet I am not by this acquitted; but the one who examines me is the Lord. Therefore do not go on passing judgment before the time, but wait until the Lord comes who will both bring to light the things hidden in the darkness and disclose the motives of men's hearts; and then each man's praise will come to him from God."*

KEY PRINCIPLE: The motive of the leader is very important.

UNDERSTAND
This passage indicates that God looks upon the motives of those in leadership or a "stewardship" position. In biblical times, a steward was someone who was given authority and/or care of something that he/she did not own. Those of us who are followers of Jesus must look upon our leadership opportunities as a trust of stewardship from God. We are to take this responsibility very seriously.

People have a variety of motives for wanting to lead or influence others. For some, the whole issue is pride. They see a leadership role as leading to recognition, accolades and praise. Others pursue a leadership role because the position may offer them the opportunity to promote a personal agenda. For some, the motive is simply power. To some people, power is everything.

The motives underlying a leader's actions will eventually become known. It is possible to conceal one's motives temporarily. Generally, the size of the group being led has a relationship to the length of time leading to exposure of the leader's motives. In a situation where the group being led is very small and has daily contact with the leader, the exposure time will usually be very short. In a situation where the group being led is very large and few have close contact with the leader, the exposure time can be lengthy. Nevertheless, in either case the leader's motives will eventually emerge. Followers are more likely to follow a leader when they believe that the leader's motives are noble and in their best interests. Jesus Christ, our greatest model for leadership, had selfless motives for leading. He subordinated His own desires, interests and safety to fulfill the will of God the Father. He stated: "not my will, but thine be done."

DIG DEEPER
1 Samuel 16:1-7; 1 Corinthians 4:9-13; Matthew 26:39

APPLY
Do I have the right motives for desiring to lead others? Am I willing to sacrifice my own personal agenda in order to care for the welfare of those being led?

PRAY
"Dear Lord, I confess that I must deal with my selfish motives for desiring to lead others. Please give me the faith to allow You to give me the right motives."

Day 11

SERVANT/LEADERS RECEIVE COUNSEL

"In abundance of counselors there is victory"
Proverbs 24:6

OBSERVE
Proverbs 24:3-6

> *"By wisdom a house is built, and by understanding it is established; and by knowledge the rooms are filled with all precious and pleasant riches. A wise man is strong and a man of knowledge increases power; for by wise guidance you will wage war; and in abundance of counselors there is victory."*

Luke 14:28-31

> *"For which one of you, when he wants to build a tower, does not first sit down and calculate the cost, to see if he has enough to complete it? Otherwise, when he has laid a foundation, and is not able to finish, all who observe it begin to ridicule him, saying, 'This man began to build and was not able to finish.' Or what king, when he sets out to meet another king in battle, will not first sit down and take counsel whether he is strong enough with ten thousand men to encounter the one coming against him with twenty thousand?"*

KEY PRINCIPLE: Effective leaders seek counsel from others.

UNDERSTAND
In these biblical references we see the importance of the leader seeking counsel before taking action or during the planning process. The Bible is indicating that effective leaders will not develop a vision or plan in a vacuum, without the participation of others.

Often the leader is unaware of the perspective or information held by the followers. Ideally, a leader should be aware of the problems, challenges and opportunities that the followers face.

Being "visionary" is one of the traits recognized as essential to leadership. Those who have studied leaders who are visionary have noted that they do not develop their vision alone. Visionary leaders have the wisdom to include ideas and insights from other in developing their vision. They consult a variety of people and sources of information, including peers, competitors and subordinates. In large organizations, people at the operating level who are actually doing the job often know more about problem solving than the bosses at the top. Children can give their parents important insights about their life at school. Effective leaders recognize that wise counsel does not always come from older or "superior" sages.

Developing a vision or a plan for the future should involve a lot of hard work and preparation. It is easier to sit down and do this task alone. But consulting others, including the followers, will result in a better plan with more "buy-in" by those who will implement it.

DIG DEEPER
Proverbs 15:22; Proverbs 12:15; Proverbs 1:5

APPLY
Do I aggressively seek out counsel in developing my vision or plan? Who should I bring within my sphere of counsel in my present circumstances?

PRAY
"Dear Lord, please give me the wisdom and humility to seek counsel as I pursue leadership. Give me the wisdom to select people who can give me the insights I need to consider."

Day 12

SERVANT/LEADERS PURSUE ENDURANCE

"By faith he left Egypt, not fearing the wrath of the king; for he endured, as seeing Him who is unseen."
Hebrews 11:27

OBSERVE
Hebrews 11:24-29

> *"By faith Moses, when he had grown up, refused to be called the son of Pharaoh's daughter; choosing rather to endure ill treatment with the people of God, than to enjoy the passing pleasures of sin; considering the reproach of Christ greater riches than the treasures of Egypt; for he was looking to the reward. By faith he left Egypt, not fearing the wrath of the king; for he endured, as seeing Him who is unseen. By faith he kept the Passover and the sprinkling of the blood, so that he who destroyed the first-born might not touch them. By faith they passed through the Red Sea as though they were passing through dry land; and the Egyptians, when they attempted it, were drowned."*

Exodus 9:13-17

> *"Then the Lord said to Moses, 'Rise up early in the morning and stand before Pharaoh and say to him, Thus says the Lord, the God of the Hebrews, Let my people go, that they may serve Me. For this time I will send all My plagues on you and your servants and your people, so that you may know that there is no one like Me in all the earth. But, indeed, for this cause I have allowed you to remain, in order to show you My power,*

and in order to proclaim My name through all the earth. Still you exalt yourself against My people by not letting them go.'"

KEY PRINCIPLE: Effective leaders do not give up easily. They endure and eventually experience victory or success.

UNDERSTAND

Biblical leaders continued to pursue their goals amid rejection, opposition and resistance. Moses continued to ask Pharaoh to "let his people go" even though Pharaoh "hardened his heart" after each of the many miraculous plagues brought against Egypt. Eventually, he successfully led his people out of Egypt. Joseph persevered and continued to trust God even though he was unjustly thrown in prison. He pursued excellence during his undeserved punishment and eventually rose to the most powerful leadership position in his world. The Apostle Paul continued to spread the Gospel of Jesus Christ even though he suffered rejection, imprisonment and beatings.

One of the common character traits of effective leaders is that of perseverance. Leaders continue to pursue their objectives even when they experience failure. Abraham Lincoln lost more elections than he won. Thomas Edison failed hundreds of times in his attempt to produce practical light from electricity. Neither of these men "threw in the towel." They are typical of admired leaders.

The clear model of leadership in the Bible always includes the character trait of endurance. Acts of leadership are almost always met with resistance. One of the traits that distinguish true leadership is their determination to not succumb to that resistance. True leaders endure.

DIG DEEPER
Romans 5:3-5; 2 Corinthians 6:1-10; 2 Timothy 2:8-13

APPLY

What goals or objectives have I given up on when I should have endured? What goal or project am I facing at the present time where endurance is needed?

PRAY

"Lord, please give me the diligence and courage to endure as I call upon you to help me to seize the initiative to lead."

Day 13

SERVANT/LEADERS MENTOR AND DELEGATE AUTHORITY TO PEOPLE OF CHARACTER

"Moses chose able men out of all Israel, and made them heads over the people."
Exodus 18:25

OBSERVE
Exodus 18:13-25

> "And it came about the next day that Moses sat to judge the people, and the people stood about Moses from the morning until the evening. Now when Moses' father-in-law saw all that he was doing for the people, he said 'What is this thing that you are doing for the people? Why do you alone sit as judge and all the people stand about you from morning until evening?' And Moses said to his father-in-law 'Because the people come to me to inquire of God. When they have a dispute, it comes to me, and I judge between a man and his neighbor and make known the statutes of God and His laws.' And Moses' father-in-law said to him, 'The thing that you are doing is not good. You will surely wear out, both yourself and these people who are with you, for the task is too heavy for you; you cannot do it alone. Now listen to me: I shall give you counsel and God be with you. You be the people's representative before God, and you bring the disputes to God, then teach them the statutes and the laws, and make known to them the way in which thy are to walk, and the work they are to do. Furthermore, you shall select out of all the people able men who fear God, men of truth, those who hate dishonest gain; and you shall place them over them, as leaders of thousands, of hundreds, of fifties and of tens. And let them judge the people at all times; and let it be that every major

dispute they will bring to you, but every minor dispute they themselves will judge. So it will be easier for you, and they will bear the burden with you. If you do this thing and God so commands you, then you will be able to endure and all these people also will go to their place in peace.' So Moses listened to his father-in-law, and did all that he had said. And Moses chose able men out of all Israel, and made them heads over the people, leaders of thousands, of hundreds, of fifties and of tens."

KEY PRINCIPLE: Leaders carefully choose and prepare delegated leaders.

UNDERSTAND

In this biblical story of leadership, we see Moses being bogged down with leadership responsibility to the point of becoming ineffective. His father-in-law counsels him to carefully select men of character to help him. Two principles emerge as important in this process. First, Moses is encouraged to "teach them the statutes and the laws, and make known to them the way in which they are to walk, and the work they are to do." Secondly, Moses is told to select "able men who fear God, men of truth (or integrity), those who hate dishonest gain." This clearly promotes a selection that duplicates the mandate of character outlined in our text from 1 Timothy 3 that we studied on Day Eight.

In other words, a leader should prepare a group of people for leadership through training; and then carefully select from this group people that have the necessary character traits to support their knowledge and preparation.

Many people, who have excellent leadership character and skills themselves, fail in the overall job of leadership by neglecting the biblical principle of multiplying themselves through others. Jesus recognized that even He must prepare others to help Him spread the Gospel. He selected and prepared His disciples to expand his own sphere of influence. He sent them out while He was still here on earth, and commanded them to continue their leadership after he was gone.

Effective leaders prepare others to help them. They also anticipate the future and establish a succession plan to continue their influence after they themselves are unable to carry on.

DIG DEEPER
2 Timothy 2:1-2; Deuteronomy 31:1-13; Matthew 13:16-19

APPLY
Have I selected and prepared qualified people of character to lead? If my life came to an end this week, would there be anyone to continue my legacy?

PRAY
"Dear Lord, please give me the wisdom to select at least one person and then prepare them for leadership."

Day 14

DOERS OF THE WORD

"But prove yourselves doers of the word, and not merely hearers who delude themselves. For if anyone is a hearer of the word and not a doer, he is like a man who looks at his natural face in a mirror; for once he has looked at himself and gone away, he has immediately forgotten what kind of person he was. But one who looks intently at the perfect law, the law of liberty, and abides by it, not having become a forgetful hearer but an effectual doer, this man shall be blessed in what he does."
James 1:22-25

Looking back over the week, I learned . . .

Day 8 - Leadership involves character.

Day 9 - Leaders recognize great opportunities and seize the initiative.

Day 10 - Motive is important in leadership.

Day 11 - Servant/Leaders receive counsel.

Day 12 - Servant/Leaders pursue endurance.

Day 13 - Servant/Leaders mentor and delegate.

Journal Space

Lord, I am grateful for you teaching me the following:

Lord, I plan on being a leader who follows God by:

I have questions about:

Day 15

SERVANT/LEADERSHIP INVOLVES SPECIFIC CHARACTER TRAITS

"And the Lord was with Joseph, so he became a successful man."
Genesis 39:2

OBSERVE
Genesis 39:2-9

> *"And the Lord was with Joseph, so he became a successful man. And he was in the house of his master, the Egyptian. Now his master saw that the Lord was with him and how the Lord caused all that he did to prosper in his hand. So Joseph found favor in his sight, and became his personal servant; and he made him overseer over his house, and all that he owned he put in his charge. And it came about that from the time he made him overseer in his house, and over all that he owned, the Lord blessed the Egyptian's house on account of Joseph; thus the Lord's blessing was upon all that he owned, in the house and in the field. So he left everything he owned in Joseph's charge; and with him there he did not concern himself with anything except the food which he ate. Now Joseph was handsome in form and appearance. And it came about after these events that his master's wife looked with desire at Joseph, and she said, 'Lie with me.' But he refused and said to his master's wife 'Behold with me here, my master does not concern himself with anything in the house, and he has put all that he owns in my charge. . . How then could I do this great evil, and sin against God?' "*

KEY PRINCIPLE: Specific character traits lead to success as a leader.

UNDERSTAND

Joseph was successful in managing the household of Potiphar, a high official in Egypt, the most powerful nation and culture of his time. He arrived in Egypt as a slave but soon rose to a position of great responsibility and power. Little is said about his abilities or skills in this brief overview of his rise to power. Much is said about his character. He had the trust of his master.

His character was tested in one of the most trying temptations of a single man. His master's wife made herself available to him. His refusal statement says much about his character. He referred to the unlimited trust that his master had placed in him. Then he stated: "How then could I do this great evil, and sin against God?" This statement not only explains his loyalty to his master, it also illustrated his devotion to God. His response of literally running from this great temptation says volumes about his character. He recognized his own weakness and acted with discipline, integrity and resolve.

Joseph fell victim to the anger of a spurned woman. He was unjustly placed in prison. But even there he again rose to a position of leadership. Soon he had responsibility and power while a prisoner. He demonstrated perseverance, diligence and continued loyalty. Eventually, God provided another opportunity for leadership. He became the most powerful person, save Pharaoh, in the most powerful nation and culture in the ancient world. All because of his faith in God and his consistent life of proven character.

DIG DEEPER

Psalms 105:16-22; Proverbs 2:6-9; Hebrews 11:8

APPLY

When planning a project involving my leadership, do I think in terms of character?

PRAY

"Lord, please help me to focus on the concept of character as I pursue your principles of leadership."

Day 16

HOW DOES INTEGRITY RELATE TO LEADERSHIP?

"For Ezra had set his heart to study the law of the Lord, and to practice it."
Ezra 7:10

OBSERVE
Ezra 7:10-21

> *"For Ezra had set his heart to study the law of the Lord, and to practice it, and to teach His statutes and ordinances in Israel. Now this is the copy of the decree which King Artaxerxes gave to Ezra the priest, the scribe, learned in the words of the commandments of the lord and His statutes to Israel: 'Artaxerxes, king of kings, to Ezra the priest, the scribe of the law of the God of heaven, perfect peace. And now, I have issued a decree that any of the people of Israel and their priests and the Levites in my kingdom who are willing to go to Jerusalem, may go with you. Forasmuch as you are sent by the king and his seven counselors to inquire concerning Judah and Jerusalem according to the law of your God which is in your hand, and to bring the silver and gold, which the king and his counselors have freely offered to the God of Israel, whose dwelling is in Jerusalem, with all the silver and gold which you shall find in the whole province of Babylon, along with the freewill offering of the people and of the priests, who offered willingly for the house of their God which is in Jerusalem . . .' "*

KEY PRINCIPLE: Integrity leads to trust. Trust is necessary for leadership to occur.

UNDERSTAND

In this passage of scripture we find an amazing story of trust and leadership. Ezra had established a trust relationship with King Artaxerxes. So much so that the king gave Ezra the golden articles that had been previously taken from the temple in Jerusalem. He gave Ezra their care and custody and allowed him to lead a contingent of Israelis back to Jerusalem.

The word integrity comes from the root *integer* meaning whole or undivided. In mathematics, it is the opposite of a fraction. Integrity is defined as:

> *An unimpaired condition; soundness; adherence to a code of moral, artistic, or other values; the state of being complete or undivided.*

Therefore someone with integrity is whole rather than divided. A person of integrity performs actions that match his/her stated beliefs or values. Someone with integrity is *one person* rather than several personalities based on the present circumstance. Integrity is the opposite of duplicity.

When a leader is known for having strong beliefs and most importantly *living* by them, he or she becomes predictable in the sense of providing guidance. People have confidence in following someone who is consistent in this regard. This consistency allows the followers to predict how the leader would respond to a given situation even when the leader is not present and unavailable for counsel. This predictability gives the followers the confidence to make the correct decision on their own.

Integrity is basic to **sustained** effective leadership. It is a threshold ("make or break") issue. A leader without integrity can lead for a short time; but eventually his/her lack of integrity will become exposed. At that point effective leadership begins to diminish.

Every phase of leadership involves trust. There must be trust that the leader is leading in the right direction. There must be trust that he or she will support the actions of the followers as long as they operate within the agreed upon parameters; trust that he or she will keep commitments. And perhaps most importantly, trust that his or her motives are not self centered but rather altruistic – with the interests of the team in first place.

Integrity is where we must begin in discussing the foundations of character for those interested in leadership. Integrity makes one complete, undivided, and unimpaired. Integrity makes someone believable–or trustworthy. Trust is the link between integrity and leadership. From a utilitarian perspective, one interested in leadership should pursue integrity, even if he or she does not value the moral implications. Integrity earns trust. Trust is necessary to sustained leadership. It is just that simple.

DIG DEEPER
1 Kings 9:3-5; 1 Chronicles 29:15-19; Proverbs 11:3

APPLY
How can I improve my commitment to integrity? What steps can I take this week to begin sharpening my character in reference to integrity?

PRAY
"Dear Lord, please give me the wisdom and humility to accurately reflect upon my character in regard to integrity. Help me strengthen my character."

Day 17

HOW DOES COURAGE RELATE TO LEADERSHIP?

"Be strong and courageous"
Joshua 1:6

OBSERVE
Joshua 1:5-9

> *"No man will be able to stand before you all the days of your life. Just as I have been with Moses, I will be with you; I will not fail you or forsake you. Be strong and **courageous**, for you shall give this people possession of the land which I swore to their fathers to give to them. Only be strong and very **courageous**; be careful to do according to all the law which Moses My servant commanded you; do not turn from it to the right or to the left, so that you may have success wherever you go. This book of the law shall not depart from your mouth, but you shall meditate on it day and night, so that you may be careful to do according to all that is written it; for then you will make your way prosperous, and then you will have success. Have I not commanded you? Be strong and **courageous**! Do not tremble or be dismayed, for the Lord your God is with you wherever you go."*

KEY PRINCIPLE: Effective leaders have courage to put their beliefs into action.

UNDERSTAND
Courage has been defined as the characteristic that allows someone to overcome a fear in order to do what one chooses to do. It implies firmness of mind and willpower in the face of danger or extreme difficulty. Integrity without courage can result in good intentions and beliefs without the consistency of action.

Joshua was selected to take the leadership position of the nation of Israel. In this passage God's initial instructions to Joshua are recorded. In this brief narrative, God tells Joshua three times to be courageous. God connects this character trait with leadership and taking the right actions. God tells Joshua to stop trembling. Leadership does have certain fears attached to it. The fear of failing and the fear of rejection are two of the most common fears connected with leadership.

In a very real sense, courage cannot exist outside the presence of fear. An act or decision that involves no fear may be commendable, admirable, and even right or just; but it cannot involve courage. The very essence of the concept implies the ability to overcome an anxiety or dread that inhibits a person's behavior. Courage is overcoming fear.

One of the hallmarks of great leaders is the desire to "seize the initiative." A leader is not the observer who watches things happen. The leader *makes* things happen. Seizing the initiative involves recognizing problems, seeing a window of opportunity, perceiving a vacuum of leadership and then taking action without having to be told to do so. Everyone will intersect with a great opportunity during his or her lifetime. More likely you will encounter several of them. The issue is not whether or not you will have a rendezvous with a "window of opportunity," it is whether or not you will (1) recognize it as such, and then (2) seize the initiative and jump through the "window. " This requires courage.

> *"Right is right, no matter how many are against it;*
> *Wrong is wrong no matter how many are for it."*

DIG DEEPER
2 Chronicles 15:8; 2 Chronicles 32:1-7; John 16:33

APPLY

What fears do I face in my leadership responsibilities? What can I do to overcome my fears?

PRAY

"Lord, please help me to overcome my fears and take courageous acts of leadership."

Day 18

HOW DOES DISCIPLINE RELATE TO LEADERSHIP?

". . .everyone who competes in the games exercises self-control in all things."
1 Corinthians 9:25

OBSERVE
1 Corinthians 9:24-27

> *"Do you not know that those who run in a race all run, but only one receives the prize? Run in such a way that you may win. And everyone who competes in the games (Olympics) exercises self-control in all things. They then do it to receive a perishable wreath, but we an imperishable. Therefore I run in such a way, as not without aim; I box in such a way, as not beating the air; but I buffet my body and make it my slave, lest possibly, after I have preached to others, I myself should be disqualified."*

KEY PRINCIPLE: Effective leaders practice self-control (discipline).

UNDERSTAND
The selected passage is part of a sort of resume that the Apostle Paul is giving the Corinthians to establish his rights as a minister/leader. As part of that "resume" he also includes this factor of discipline or self-control which, if not exercised, will be the grounds for disqualification as a leader.

The Bible establishes the principle that those in positions of leadership shall be held to a higher level of accountability than others. Jesus warned that those who would lead children in the wrong direction should be cast into the ocean with a millstone around their neck (Matthew 18:1-10). In James 3:1, we are admonished to not seek the position of teacher (some leadership positions rise to the teacher role) in that "we shall incur a stricter judgment." God did not allow the great leader Moses to enter the Promised Land because he did not exercise self-control and follow God's specific command about bringing water out of a rock. The Bible clearly establishes a link between leadership and discipline or self-control.

When an individual attempts to lead, he or she is asking those being led to grant control of their lives (at least on a limited basis) to them. Most people relinquish control of their lives to others rather hesitantly, to say the least. When they do, it is to someone who has demonstrated a measure of success in self-control. This is because there will always be some uncertainty of outcome—some hazard, even if ever so slight. This issue of granting control to the leader is what makes discipline necessary to leadership.

Discipline is not pursued for its own sake. Discipline is an unnatural character trait that is tolerated because it is a precursor to other desirable outcomes. Curiously, the practice of discipline often leads to embracing it. This is not because it is natural, but due to its rewards. For example, studies have shown that people who exercise the discipline of preparing written goals (even a daily "to do list") accomplish much more than those who do not.

It has been observed that those who are the most successful in developing discipline follow a basic principle--the principle of planning gradual and progressively more difficult challenges. In other words they begin modestly and celebrate realistic and achievable goals. Then they move on to moderate and eventually more difficult objectives. Most of us err in taking a step larger or more difficult than we should and then give up when we experience defeat.

DIG DEEPER
Proverbs 25:28; Colossians 2:5; Daniel 1:8

APPLY

What are some practical ways that I can demonstrate discipline (self-control) in my life? What are three modest goals that I can begin working toward this week?

PRAY

"Lord, please help me to determine some realistic goals that will involve self-control; and then give me the inner strength to achieve them.

Day 19

HOW DOES LOYALTY RELATE TO LEADERSHIP?

"For I, too, am a man under authority, with soldiers under me; and I say to this one, 'Go!' and he goes. . ."
Matthew 8:9

OBSERVE
Matthew 8:5-10

> *"And when He had entered Capernaum, a centurion came to Him, entreating Him, and saying, 'Lord, my servant is lying paralyzed at home, suffering great pain.' And He said to him, 'I will come and heal him.' But the centurion answered and said, 'Lord, I am not worthy for You to come under my roof, but just say the word, and my servant will be healed. For I, too, am a man **under** authority, with soldiers under me; and I say to this one, 'go!' and he goes, and to another 'come!' and he comes, and to my slave 'do this!' And he does it.' Now when Jesus heard this, He marveled, and said to those who were following, 'Truly I say to you, I have not found such great faith with anyone in Israel.'"*

KEY PRINCIPLE: Effective leaders place themselves under legitimate authority, practicing loyalty.

UNDERSTAND
God placed this story in the Bible to teach us an important lesson about leadership and authority. It is not just a story about amazing faith and a miraculous healing; it is also a lesson about leadership. The centurion first of all recognized that Jesus was under authority when he stated, "I, too, am a man under authority." Then he connected the position of being **under** authority as empowering a person **with** authority. The centurion's great faith in Jesus was

connected to his recognition that Jesus was under the authority of The Father, God Almighty. He explained this by pointing to his position of centurion under the authority of Caesar giving him strong authority.

The importance of submitting to legitimate authority must be very important to God. He repeats this theme throughout the Bible. As one submits to his or her authority, in a real sense they are letting authority flow through them. Said another way, if leaders desire authority, they must submit to it. When someone complains that they are experiencing a problem with subordinates failing to recognize his or her authority, chances are they are not living in submission to the authority over them. Followers need a clear example of how to follow.

The character trait of loyalty means the leader submits to the authority above him or her. Authority is essential to effective leadership. Therefore, the character trait of loyalty must be pursued and valued by all those seeking to lead. This important virtue places one *under* the flow of power. As a result, the power flows through them. The leader must demonstrate to his or her followers the discipline of following. This act of loyalty teaches others how to follow.

This principle demonstrates that in order to lead, *one must follow*.

Tomorrow we will examine the Biblical exception to this principle.

DIG DEEPER
1 Peter 2:13-15; Romans 13:1-7

APPLY
Where have I failed to comply with this very important principle to submit to authority? What must I do to correct my behavior and attitude in order to be granted authority?

PRAY

"Lord, please reveal to me where I have failed to comply with your requirement to submit to legitimate authority."

Day 20

WHAT IS THE CORRECT ACTION TO TAKE WHEN THE AUTHORITY OVER ME CONFLICTS WITH SPECIFIC DIRECTION FROM GOD?

"But Peter and apostles answered and said, 'We must obey God rather than men."
Acts 5:29

OBSERVE
Acts 5:25-29

> *"But someone came and reported to them, 'Behold, the men whom you put in prison are standing in the temple and teaching the people!' Then the captain went along with the officers and proceeded to bring them back without violence (for they were afraid of the people, lest they should be stoned). And when they had brought them, they stood them before the Council. And the high priest questioned them, saying 'We gave you strict orders not to continue teaching in this name, and behold, you have filled Jerusalem with your teaching, and intend to bring this man's blood upon us.' But Peter and the apostles answered and said, 'We must obey God rather than men.'"*

KEY PRINCIPLE: Loyalty and submission to God overrules submission to his delegated authority in human leaders.

UNDERSTAND
There is one important exception to submitting to authority and it involves the issue of principle. When one is asked to deviate from an important moral principle or violate the law, the answer must be "No." **However, these situations are usually rare and one must use**

extreme discretion in negotiating these difficult waters. Even a well-meaning error can have severe repercussions and undermine your own authority.

In refusing to submit to authority, one must first determine that the request actually violates a *principle* and not just a *preference*. The key focus should be classifying the issue correctly. Most of us tend to hastily classify something we object to as a violation of principle. A careful analysis of the situation will often reveal the issue is one of personal preference rather than principle. This distinction is of utmost importance, for refusing to submit to authority when it is not an issue of principle will result in the loss of power.

Principles that justify disobeying or subverting authority must be based on some tangible precept. A violation of the law or the breaking of widely accepted social standards, such as the time tested "Ten Commandments," would qualify. The nebulous plea of "conscience" alone cannot override the command to submit.

Of course, when a subordinate refuses to follow the unlawful or immoral direction of his or her boss, there is the possibility of reprisal. Usually this will *not* occur since the superior will not want immoral or illegal direction to become public. But even though some negative fallout does occur, your integrity is preserved and even the misguided superior has learned about an important and valuable component of your character. Although he or she may be angry and frustrated at the time, this personal experience can be the basis for increased trust in the long run. That same immoral superior may well turn to you when he or she really wants someone to trust.

People have argued that this idea of loyalty does not apply if their boss is "unreasonable." The notion of being *unreasonable* involves a value judgment that does not qualify as a *principled* excuse. In 1 Peter 2:18 we read: *"Submit (to an employer or superior), not only to those who are kind and good; but also to those who are unreasonable."*

Refusing to submit to authority based solely upon a subjective evaluation of the person in authority or the issue at point must be seen for what it is--disloyalty and disobedience.

Parents who demonstrate rebellious attitudes toward authority should not be surprised if their children grow up resisting authority.

However, being loyal does not mean becoming a sycophant or a "yes man." Often the most powerful demonstration of loyalty or friendship is "wounding" or constructively criticizing a friend in love, as stated in the Proverbs passage below.

DIG DEEPER
1 Peter 2:18-21; Proverbs 27:6; Acts 23:1-5.

APPLY
When have I rationalized my insubordination to legitimate authority by convincing myself I would be compromising a command from God when it was actually a strong personal preference?

PRAY
"Lord, please help me to recognize when I resist your direction through the authority you have placed over me. Give me the wisdom to discern between my personal preference and specific principles or commands from you."

Day 21

DOERS OF THE WORD

"But prove yourselves doers of the word, and not merely hearers who delude themselves. For if anyone is a hearer of the word and not a doer, he is like a man who looks at his natural face in a mirror; for once he has looked at himself and gone away, he has immediately forgotten what kind of person he was. But one who looks intently at the perfect law, the law of liberty, and abides by it, not having become a forgetful hearer but an effectual doer, this man shall be blessed in what he does."
James 1:22-25

Looking back over the week, I learned . . .

Day 15 - Servant/Leadership involves specific character traits.

Day 16 - How does integrity relate to leadership?

Day 17 - How does courage relate to leadership?

Day 18 - How does discipline relate to leadership?

Day 19 - How does loyalty relate to leadership?

Day 20 - When loyalty to authority conflicts with God's direction.

Journal Space

Lord, I am grateful for you teaching me the following:

Lord, I plan on being a leader who follows God by:

I have questions about:

Day 22

HOW DOES DILIGENCE RELATE TO LEADERSHIP?

". . . He who leads, with diligence."
Romans 12:8

OBSERVE
Romans 12:3-11

> *"For through the grace given to me I say to every man among you not to think more highly of himself than he ought to think; but to think so as to have sound judgment, as God has allotted to each a measure of faith. For just as we have many members in one body and all the members do not have the same function, so we, who are many, are one body in Christ, and individually members one of another. And since we have gifts that differ according to the grace given to us, let each exercise them accordingly: if prophecy, according to the proportion of his faith; if service, in his serving; or he who teaches in his teaching; or he who exhorts, in his exhortation; he who gives, with liberality; **he who leads, with diligence;** he who shows mercy, with cheerfulness. Let love be without hypocrisy. Abhor what is evil; cling to what is good. Be devoted to one another in brotherly love; give preference to one another in honor; **not lagging behind in diligence**, fervent in spirit, serving the Lord."*

KEY PRINCIPLE: Diligence is a powerful character trait necessary to leadership.

UNDERSTAND
Our Biblical text for today outlines some of the basic gifts given to us to glorify God. Each person has a unique combination of these gifts. Some Bible scholars believe that everyone has a measure of

leadership, since true leadership is being an influence in someone's life; and we are all called to that responsibility. At the end of the text we are admonished to be diligent in exercising these gifts. But, **leading** is the only gift that is singled out with a direct link with diligence.

Diligence in one's work is highly desired by many, especially those hiring workers and employers. Yet it is becoming more difficult to find. During the last several decades there has been erosion of the "work ethic." Some have even berated it as "old fashioned" and describe workers who have this trait as naive and foolish.

In the early days of America, a person worked hard and with devotion to achieving excellence in his or her craft because it was moral and admirable. Taking pride in one's work was held up as a desirable attitude--a noble course to pursue. Diligence was actually a component of religious life. It was a means of demonstrating one's piety and commitment to faith. Work was viewed as a "calling," and a way to bring honor to God.

In the Bible, followers of Jesus Christ are urged to work with all diligence as a clear manifestation of their true faith. This character trait is described in the Bible as not only working hard when being observed by others or one's immediate supervisor, but also when no one is looking. In this sense it is described as a virtue that will ultimately reap favorable results because it is the "right" thing to do.

Diligence not only involves working hard. It also involves the pursuit of excellence. This is indeed a noble effort. The phrase, "pursuit of excellence" demonstrates that in a sense one never arrives. As one level of excellence is achieved, it enables one to reach for an even higher level of excellence.

The leader has the primary responsibility of "sowing the seeds" of excellence in his or her followers. Once again the most effective way to do this is to model excellence and reward those who embrace it. Talk is cheap. Actions powerfully communicate this ethic. The leader must demonstrate commitment to excellence in his or her personal life as well as deliberately and publicly giving positive reinforcement to those who follow. He or she must keep focus on this important concept.

Diligence is a necessary component in the effective leader's character. It makes it possible for the leader to develop to his or her full potential. More importantly, diligence on the part of the leader becomes contagious. It germinates a **culture** that can provide an environment where hard work and excellence become a way of life.

DIG DEEPER
Ephesians 6:5-8; Proverbs 12:27; Hebrews 6:9-12

APPLY
Do I achieve much satisfaction and fulfillment from my work? I am committed to doing my best even when alone and unobserved? Do I present a strong role model of diligence to those I desire to influence?

PRAY
"Dear Lord, help me deepen my commitment to the character trait of diligence. Help me to pursue excellence and not merely acceptable standards."

Day 23

HOW DOES HUMILITY RELATE TO LEADERSHIP?

"Now the man Moses was very humble, more than any man who was on the face of the earth."
Numbers 12:3

OBSERVE
Numbers 12:1-8

> *"Then Miriam and Aaron spoke against Moses because of the Cushite woman whom he had married (for he had married a Cushite woman); and they said, 'Has the Lord indeed spoken only through Moses? Has He not spoken through us as well?' And the Lord heard it. (Now the man Moses was very humble, more than any man who was on the face of the earth). And suddenly the Lord said to Moses and Aaron and to Miriam, 'You three come out to the tent of meeting.' So, the three of them came out. Then the Lord came down in a pillar of cloud and stood at the doorway of the tent, and He called Aaron and Miriam. When they had both come forward, He said, 'Hear now my words; if there is a prophet among you. I, the Lord, shall make Myself known to him in a vision. I shall speak with him in a dream. Not so, with My servant Moses. He is faithful in all My household; with him I speak mouth to mouth. Even openly, and not in dark sayings. And he beholds the form of the Lord. Why then were you not afraid to speak against My servant, against Moses?' "*

KEY PRINCIPLE: Humility is requirement of being a powerful leader.

UNDERSTAND
Moses is known, almost universally, as one of the greatest leaders of all time. He was chosen by God to lead the Israelites out of Egypt.

God gave us the law through him. He was even empowered by God to perform mighty miracles. Yet, we read in the text that he was the humblest man on earth at that time.

Of all the character traits we will discuss in this study, humility is perhaps the one most apt to be overlooked as supportive of strong leadership. At first blush, humility may seem to be inconsistent with strong conviction or the courageous risk-taking that is necessary for leadership. Humility has a perverted meaning to many. Webster's dictionary defines this character trait as, "*not proud or haughty; not arrogant.*" Being haughty or arrogant is dysfunctional to inspiring leadership. People resist following someone with a closed mind to their ideas or suggestions. On the contrary, they enjoy contributing their insights to someone seeking their support.

True humility makes someone teachable. We learn and develop good judgment in two basic ways: (1) By receiving information from others (either reading or listening); (2) By learning from our own mistakes. Both of these methods require humility. Humility allows one to have an "open mind." People with humility look upon life as an experience of continued learning. Humility is a precursor to good listening. It also takes humility to admit when you are wrong. This recognition can lead one to be open to new ideas, different insights and even opposing opinions.

In order to be an effective leader, one must draw on the expertise of those he or she is leading. The failure to recognize this basic principle of leadership is the most common cause of bad decisions by those in authority. Developing a vision for the future should involve receiving input and suggestions from others. Often in large organizations, people at the lowest level have the most information on a specific subject. A wise servant/leader will establish a climate where others feel free to offer their expertise and assistance. Parents also need to learn about the world that their children are facing. All of this takes humility.

Humility is also a precursor to compassion. It has been said that people do not care about what you know until they know how much you care. When humility is exercised, the leader is provided more insight, more assistance and most importantly, more admiration. Although not widely accepted as such, humility is absolutely mandatory for great leadership.

DIG DEEPER
Matthew 11:29; Proverbs 11:2; Acts 20:16-21

APPLY
Do I give undivided attention to those seeking my counsel? Do I recognize that those with less experience, skills or status may have something to contribute? When I experience failure or unrealized goals, do I recognize that I have at least some of the responsibility for that failure? Have I developed the willingness to admit when I am wrong?

PRAY
"Dear Lord, please help me to pursue true humility. Help me to see the value of those you have put into my life. Give me the ability to listen to others, recognize and admit my failures. Help me to think of others rather than myself."

Day 24

HOW DOES OPTIMISM RELATE TO LEADERSHIP?

"If there is any excellence and if anything worthy of praise, let your mind dwell on these things."
Philippians 4:8

OBSERVE
Philippians 4:6-8

> *"Be anxious for nothing, but in everything by prayer and supplication with thanksgiving let your requests be made known to God. And the peace of God, which surpasses all comprehension, shall guard your hearts and your minds in Christ Jesus. Finally, brethren, whatever is true, whatever is honorable, whatever is right, whatever is pure, whatever is lovely, whatever is of good repute, if there is any excellence and if anything worthy of praise, let your mind dwell on these things."*

KEY PRINCIPLE: Effective leaders display a "realistic" optimism.

UNDERSTAND
David was one of the most prominent leaders in the Bible. Before he became King he had a confrontation that rocketed him to fame and respect throughout Israel. His battle with the Philistine giant, Goliath, is well known. In that amazing story from 1 Samuel 17, David displayed remarkable optimism as he approached a seemingly impossible foe. In his conversation with King Saul before the battle he said, "The Lord who delivered me from the paw of the lion and from the paw of the bear, He will deliver me from the hand of this Philistine."

People began to follow him even before he became king. Throughout his life he led soldiers into battle, many times against unfavorable odds. He developed a band of followers referred to as "David's mighty men." He developed such a strong loyalty among his followers, that at one point many of them risked their lives just to get him a drink of water that his desired from a particular well (2 Samuel 23).

People prefer following someone who demonstrates that they believe the objective can and probably will be met. On the contrary, they are demoralized by a leader who indicates, in even subtle ways, that they doubt the mission can or will be accomplished. It is human nature to avoid or put little effort into something perceived futile or impossible. There is a danger in optimism. Optimistic leadership does not mean putting a blind eye to obstacles. A leader who denies or ignores real or perceived obstacles can demoralize their followers as well. Effective leaders strike a balance of "realistic optimism." This means properly addressing obstacles without becoming consumed by them. It also means expecting the best from those you lead and aggressively searching for behavior you can reinforce with recognition and encouragement.

Perhaps the most powerful impact of a realistic optimist is that of spreading confidence and enthusiasm. The celebration of even minor victories or accomplishments is encouraging. When people are encouraged about their work their confidence begins to grow. As confidence expands, a person becomes more innovative and willing to take some risks to become more effective. This can result in an upward spiral that builds upon itself. Enthusiasm is contagious.
Successful people are those who enjoy what they are doing. When work is fun and rewarding, people not only work harder, they work smarter. Work becomes a channel to fulfillment. Work is not just viewed as a means to an end. It can become a favorable end in itself. That is the challenge of leadership--to make work fun and fulfilling. This mandates a *realistic optimism* on the part of leadership.

A spirit of optimism creates an atmosphere that is fertile for the growth of excellence and accomplishment. Leaders will either create this nurturing climate, or one that is confining and discouraging. A leader with realistic optimism does not deny the existence of problems; he or she addresses them with a "can do" attitude. He focuses on the objectives, not the obstacles. He expects the best from his followers. He exudes confidence that they will persevere, succeed, and be victorious.

DIG DEEPER
2 Samuel 23:14-17; 1 Samuel 17:31- 49; 1 Thessalonians 5:14

APPLY
Do followers feel free to bring problem situations to my attention in matters under my leadership? Do my followers seem to enjoy working together even when confronted with major problems? Have I established ways to identify excellent behavior in my followers and give recognition to those involved in it? Do I usually face difficulties with a "can do" attitude?

PRAY
"Dear Lord, please give me the wisdom to look for things worthy of praise. Help me to not be intimidated with problems so that I lose sight of the objectives. May I encourage those within my influence by 'catching' them doing something good."

Day 25

HOW DOES DEVELOPING A STRONG BELIEF SYSTEM RELATE TO LEADERSHIP?

". . .and you know in all your hearts and in all your souls that not one word of all the good words which the Lord your God spoke concerning you has failed."
Joshua 23:14

OBSERVE
Joshua 23:14-16

> *"Now behold, today I am going the way of all the earth, and you know in all your hearts and in all your souls that not one word of all the good words which the Lord your God spoke concerning you has failed; all have been fulfilled for you, not one of them has failed. And it shall come about that just as all the good words which the Lord your God spoke to you have come upon you, so the Lord will bring upon you all the threats, until He has destroyed you from off this good land which the Lord your God has given you. When you transgress the covenant of the Lord your God, which He commanded you, and go and serve other gods, and bow down to them, then the anger of the Lord will burn against you, and you shall perish quickly from off the good land which He has given you."*

KEY PRINCIPLE: Effective leaders speak with strong conviction.

UNDERSTAND
Joshua is one of the strong leaders described in the Bible. He organized, inspired and led an army of migrating Israelites into the "Promised Land." As supreme commander of their army he led them through a series of campaigns against the people occupying the

country. This was an amazing accomplishment. People are compelled to defend their homeland. The people occupying the country had built impressive cities, fortifications and wonderful homes. Joshua's army literally drove these people from their homes and cities. Of course, the power of God was with them.

Today's passage is Joshua's farewell. In a farewell message, leaders leave their followers with what they believe is most important. Joshua spoke of his strong belief in God and His absolute reliability. One can sense his strong convictions. He believed God. He reflected on God's promises and warnings. His words left no doubt in his followers' minds about his direction to them.

Leading with doubt creates doubt. We all communicate our feelings and our attitudes in many ways. Our words are not the only indication of our thoughts. Often "body language," tone of voice or facial expressions shows more than we intend. Followers can detect doubt or reservation in a leader. When this occurs, the influence of the leader is diluted. In a sense, doubt in a leader is contagious. On the other hand, when leaders communicate with deep conviction, they are very persuasive. Strong conviction is also apparent and is likewise contagious.

True leadership involves *inspiring* people to reach their full potential. Inspiration involves penetrating to the very core of a person's being. It means somehow giving them a "fire in the belly." It motivates them to the level of emotion and passion. In order to do this, the leader must be impassioned and have conviction. Conviction gives the leader the confidence to be an example and the assurance to show the way rather than just talk about it.

The bad news is that conviction does not typically occur in a vacuum of facts. Conviction has a price. It develops as a person accumulates facts about the subject at hand. In other words, conviction requires determination and hard work. Effective leaders do the homework to define their character with some strongly held absolutes. They defy criticism, ridicule and rejection while taking a stand. They have conviction.

DIG DEEPER
Romans 8:37-39; 2 Timothy 1:12; Daniel 2:20-23

APPLY
Have I identified a set of absolutes that allow me to clearly draw the line on matters involved in my leadership? Have I identified several subject areas that are relevant to my desire to lead and have I done the research to form my belief system in those areas?

PRAY
"Dear Lord, give me the discipline to do the research necessary to develop more conviction about subjects and issues in my leadership position."

Day 26

CAN ONE CHOOSE TO FOLLOW THE ROAD TO GOOD CHARACTER?

"So choose life in order that you may live . . . by loving the Lord your God, by obeying His voice, and by holding fast to Him; for this is your life. . ."
Deuteronomy 30:19-20

OBSERVE
Deuteronomy 30:15-20

> *"See, I have set before you today life and prosperity, and death and adversity; in that I command you today to love the Lord your God, to walk in His ways and to keep His commandments and His statutes and His judgment, that you may live and multiply, and that the Lord your God may bless you in the land where you are entering to possess it. But if your heart turns away and you will not obey, but are drawn away and worship other gods and serve them, I declare to you today that you shall surely perish. You shall not prolong your days in the land where you are crossing the Jordan to enter and possess it. I call heaven and earth to witness against you today, that I have set before you life and death, the blessing and the curse. So choose life in order that you may live, you and your descendants, by loving the Lord your God, by obeying His voice, and by holding fast to Him; for this is your life and the length of your days, that you may live in the land which the Lord swore to your fathers, to Abraham, Isaac, and Jacob, to give to them."*

KEY PRINCIPLE: Whether or not to pursue the character traits given us by God in His scripture is a choice that each person must make.

UNDERSTAND

In the scripture passage for today, the great leader Moses presents a clear choice before his followers. He presents the positive results of following God's commands and warns about the consequences of not doing so. But in the end, he explains that this is a choice they must make.

In many respects we are not born equal. We are not born equal in athletic potential. We are not born equal in intellectual potential. We are not born equal in artistic potential. But we all have the same potential as far as character development. Specifically, we can all pursue the biblical character traits covered in this Bible Study series-- if we choose to do so.

Character can be defined as a consistent disciplined application of the morals one has chosen to pursue. This sentence has been divided into three parts in order to clarify its meaning.

1. *A consistent disciplined application (ethics)*
2. *of the morals (absolutes)*
3. *one has chosen to pursue. (values)*

Many use the words ethics, values and morals as if they are interchangeable. Today in public education the curriculum often includes a module referred to as "Values Clarification." In many of these courses there is an assumption that morals are relative.

Ethics: In the suggested definition *ethics* are connected to behavior. Doctors and lawyers, for example, have codes of *ethics* that require and prohibit certain specific behavior.

Morals: According to the Biblical passages in this Bible study, it is apparent that there are some absolutes.

Values: This word indicates subjectivity. What one person values greatly, another may reject as irrelevant or unimportant.

One's character can be assessed by examining the morals (absolutes) that he or she values enough to act out in their daily living (ethics).

DIG DEEPER
Joshua 24:14,15; 2 Chronicles 29:1,2

APPLY
Am I willing to deliberately choose to pursue the character traits that support effective leadership behavior? What discipline, planning and actions will be necessary to begin this process?

PRAY
"Dear Lord, please give me the inner strength that I need to choose to pursue the Biblical character traits necessary for effective leadership."

Day 27

WHAT WERE THE THREE PRIMARY STEPS THAT EZRA TOOK TO EXPERIENCE GOD'S BLESSING UPON HIS LEADERSHIP?

". . . because the good hand of his God was upon him."
Ezra 7:9

OBSERVE
Ezra 7:9,10

> "For on the first of the first month he began to go up from Babylon; and on the first of the fifth month he came to Jerusalem, because the good hand of his God was upon him. For Ezra had set his heart to study the law of the Lord, and to practice it, and to teach His statutes and ordinances in Israel. Now this is the copy of the decree which King Artaxerxes gave to Ezra the priest, the scribe, learned in the words of the commandments of the Lord and His statutes to Israel; 'Artaxerxes, king if kings, to Ezra the priest, the scribe of the law of the God of heaven, perfect peace. And now I have issued a decree that any of the people of Israel and their priests and the Levites in my kingdom who are willing to go to Jerusalem, may go with you."

KEY PRINCIPLE: God blesses the leadership of those who pursue His principles.

UNDERSTAND
We have already examined some of the leadership principles demonstrated in the life of Ezra under the topic of Integrity. Many of the people of Israel were being held captive in Babylon. Ezra was an Israeli leader who desired to return to

Jerusalem, rebuild it and settle it with Israelis who were of like mind. King Artaxerxes not only granted Ezra's desire, he gave him the treasures of Israel that had been seized and allowed him to return them to Jerusalem.

In our biblical text for today we can see three reasons that God put His hand of blessing upon Ezra.

1. He purposed in his heart to know the scriptures of God.
2. He put into practice the principles that he learned from the scriptures.
3. He taught God's principles to the people he led.

DIG DEEPER
2 Timothy 2:15; 2 Timothy 3:16; Proverbs 2:1-5

APPLY
Am I willing to make the commitment to continue studying the Word of God to obtain the wisdom it affords? Do I have the humility to daily petition God to give me the strength to live by the principles that I discover by this process? Will I have the courage to pass these principles on to others as God gives me the opportunities?

PRAY
"Dear Lord, please give me the resolve, discipline and ability to understand your principles. I humbly ask for your blessing as I put them into action."

Day 28

DOERS OF THE WORD

"But prove yourselves doers of the word, and not merely hearers who delude themselves. For if anyone is a hearer of the word and not a doer, he is like a man who looks at his natural face in a mirror; for once he has looked at himself and gone away, he has immediately forgotten what kind of person he was. But one who looks intently at the perfect law, the law of liberty, and abides by it, not having become a forgetful hearer but an effectual doer, this man shall be blessed in what he does."
James 1:22-25

Looking back over the week, I learned . . .

Day 22 - How does diligence relate to leadership?

Day 23 - How does humility relate to leadership?

Day 24 - How does optimism relate to leadership?

Day 25 - How does conviction relate to leadership?

Day 26 - Is good character a choice?

Day 27 - Why did God bless the leadership of Ezra?

Journal Space

Lord, I am grateful for you teaching me the following:

Lord, I plan on being a leader who follows God by:

I have questions about:

Day 29

WHY THESE TEN COMMANDMENTS?

"Then God spoke all these words, saying,"
Exodus 20:1

OBSERVE
Exodus 20:1-17

> *"Then God spoke all these words, saying, 'I am the Lord your God, who brought you out of the land of Egypt, out of the house of slavery. You shall have no other gods before me."*
>
> *"You shall not make for yourself an idol, or any likeness of what is in heaven above or on the earth beneath or in the water under the earth. You shall not worship them or serve them; for I, the Lord your God am a jealous God, visiting the iniquity of the fathers on the children, on the third and the fourth generations of those who hate Me, but showing lovingkindness to thousands, to those who love Me and keep My commandments."*
>
> *"You shall not take the name of the Lord your God in vain, for the Lord will not leave him unpunished who takes His name in vain."*
>
> *"Remember the Sabbath day, to keep it holy. Six days you shall labor and do all your work, but the seventh day is a Sabbath of the Lord your God; in it you shall not do any work, you or your son or your daughter, your male or your female servant or your cattle or your sojourner who stays with you. For in six days the Lord made the heavens and the earth, the sea and all that is in them, and rested on the seventh day; therefore the Lord blessed the Sabbath day and made it holy."*

"Honor your father and your mother, that your days may be prolonged in the land which the Lord your God gives you."

"You shall not murder.
You shall not commit adultery.
You shall not steal.
You shall not bear false witness against your neighbor."

"You shall not covet your neighbor's house; you shall not covet your neighbor's wife or his male servant or his female servant or his ox or his donkey or anything that belongs to your neighbor."

KEY PRINCIPLE: Leaders develop "followers" by being a good follower.

UNDERSTAND

The history of humanity provides ample evidence of our reluctance to acknowledge and obey commands. Since leaders enjoy making decisions, we seldom take pleasure in being told what to do by others. We like it even less when we are told what *not* to do! It is an unwelcome reminder that we do not have ultimate authority.

Some of today's churches may neglect the Ten Commandments, dismissing them as not God's way to salvation—which of course is true. Salvation comes through faith rather than through faultlessness (Romans 3:23; Ephesians 2:8-9). Their neglect may be one reason many church-going children have an underdeveloped sense of right and wrong. Jesus stated he did not come to "abolish the Law or the Prophets . . . but to fulfill." (Matthew 5: 17)

We would be wise to remember that this Decalogue is not called "the Ten Suggestions." These are commands and they come to us from the Lord of the Universe. All leaders are ultimately under the authority of someone, and we are prudent to humble ourselves under the authority of Almighty God.

These Ten Commandments summarize more than 600 commandments given to the Israelites by God. They have served societies for 3,000 years, providing a behavioral framework to govern respectful and responsible relationships with God and with each other. This week we will ponder these Ten Commandments. We will discover what they mean, how they make societies stronger, and how they help leaders lead better. They are not God' plan for our redemption. That comes only through faith in what Jesus Christ completed on the cross. They are how societies can become more stable and human relationships more compatible.

DIG DEEPER
Deuteronomy 6:1-3, 20-25; Psalm 19:7-11; Romans 12:2

APPLY
Do these ancient principles really apply to me in today's world? How am I responding to those in authority over me? How does respecting others increase their respect for me?

PRAY
"Dear Lord, teach me to walk humbly, obediently, and respectfully before You. Please help me show my respect for others in ways they understand and accept."

Day 30

RESPECTING GOD

"I am the LORD your God …"
Exodus 20:2

OBSERVE
Exodus 20:1-7

> *"Then God spoke all these words, saying, 'I am the Lord your God, who brought you out of the land of Egypt, out of the house of slavery.* ***You shall have no other gods before me.****'"*

> *"****You shall not make for yourself an idol*** *or any likeness of what is in heaven above or on the earth beneath or in the water under the earth. You shall not worship them or serve them; for I, the Lord your God am a jealous God, visiting the iniquity of the fathers on the children, on the third and the fourth generations of those who hate Me, but showing lovingkindness to thousands, to those who love Me and keep My commandments."*

> *"****You shall not take the name of the Lord your God in vain****, for the Lord will not leave him unpunished who takes His name in vain."*

KEY PRINCIPLE: Leaders are loyal to the authority of Almighty God.

UNDERSTAND
When we bow to God and place ourselves under the flow of His authority, we become part of something much bigger than ourselves. Such loyalty gives life meaning that transcends our pursuit of pleasure and collection of trophies. We place more importance on doing what is right and ethical. For example, a leader loyal to God will place more weight on the ultimate "good" for his or her sphere of influence.

These commands demand that our lives be centered upon God rather than upon ourselves. Worship of self is diametrically opposed to the worship of God. God requires that we demonstrate our loyalty to Him alone by abandoning our self-centered ways and giving our selfless attention to Him.

In ancient times, the name of God was invoked to signify the commitment of one party to another in an agreement, much as we do today when taking an oath of office or testifying in a court of law. In that context, the command not to misuse God's name infers that God wants those who love Him to not only treat His name with respect, but also to treat anything said or done in His name as an inviolable commitment.

Looking at the principles behind the specific commands

Commandment #1: "*You shall have no other gods before me.*"
- Key Concept: Loyalty – Choose to recognize the ultimate authority as God.
- Understand the importance of the flow of authority
- Action Step: Submit to all legitimate authority (authority that does not ask you to violate one of these 10 commands).

Commandment #2: "*You shall not make for yourself an idol*"
- Key Concept: Do not put selfish interests first (make your own gods)
- Money, materialism or anything else can become a self appointed god.
- No inflated ego
- Application step: Develop a spirit of service to others rather than self gratification.

Commandment #3: "*You shall not take the name of the Lord your God in vain.*"

- Key Concept: Keep commitments.
- History: The name of God was used to formalize agreements or commitments prior to the use of written contracts, etc. Of course it also includes cursing with God's name.
- Stabilizes relationships and reduces need for litigation
- Action Step: Become a person of your word.

DIG DEEPER
Isaiah 45:21-25; Matthew 22:37-40; Romans 13:1-7

APPLY
In what way can I show greater loyalty to God? If God works through a chain of command, how do these commands affect my relationship with other legitimate authorities in my life? What would happen to an organization, or a society, with no loyalty? How does selfless attention to God affect our relationship to other people? How can I apply these principles in my leadership style?

PRAY
"LORD my God, please help me understand how I can be more respectful and loyal to You, and more selfless in my relationships with others. Help me to become a person of my word, keeping the commitments that I choose to make."

Day 31

RESPECTING GOD'S EXAMPLE OF SABBATH REST

"Remember the Sabbath day, to keep it holy."
Exodus 20:8

OBSERVE
Exodus 20:8-11

> *"Remember the Sabbath day, to keep it holy. Six days you shall labor and do all your work, but the seventh day is a Sabbath of the Lord your God; in it you shall not do any work, you or your son or your daughter, your male or your female servant or your cattle or your sojourner who stays with you. For in six days the Lord made the heavens and the earth, the sea and all that is in them, and rested on the seventh day; therefore the Lord blessed the Sabbath day and made it holy."*

KEY PRINCIPLE: Leaders honor God when they follow His example of balancing work and rest.

UNDERSTAND
This principle has to do with maintaining a balance between work and rest. Originally this required dedicating an entire day to rest, devote oneself to honoring God and enjoying family. Many legalistic requirements proliferated over the years. Some people reacted against what they viewed as unrealistic mandates. Then the proverbial "baby was thrown out with the bath water." The basic principle is sound. Allowing one's life to get out of balance can have devastating results.

Reinforced by His personal example when He created the earth, God established a regular rhythm in our daily life that He expects us to honor. He partitioned moments into days and He grouped days into weeks. He ordained six days each week for our regular work and He set aside the seventh day as different from the others. This is to be a day of rest, a time of personal and relational renewal. He commanded that we follow this rhythmic pattern 52 times each year.

God created us. He knows our need to work—and He also knows our need to rest. He set aside this day to give balance to our lives and to encourage us to honor the example He set when he created the universe. Too often—to our eventual peril—we allow our work ethic and short-term achievement orientation to override this ancient wisdom. God calls us to create rhythm in our driven lives. He commands us to reserve room in our lifestyle for nurturing our relationship with Him and our relationships with family and friends. He expects us to tame our schedules and provide time to replenish our spiritual and emotional reservoirs.

Does this command mean that our day of rest must occur from sundown of Friday evening to the sundown of Saturday night, as in ancient times? Led by the Spirit of God, the apostle Paul (Romans 14:5-17) encourages followers of Jesus not to bog themselves down with conflicts about any specific day being more important than another, since God is LORD of all seven days each week. His words, and those of Jesus in Mark 2:27, seem to allow latitude regarding which particular day is set aside. However, the command to set aside such a day continues unchanged. It is a day for us to focus especially on following God's example and honoring Him as LORD.

Many people of faith neglect this ancient principle. The Western world is a fast paced, success-oriented society. Materialism has distorted reality for most of us. Our work ethic and achievement orientation can easily lead us to a state of imbalance. Rest, recreation and building healthy relationships can be neglected. Likewise, focusing only on the material world can lead to a neglect of the intangible aspects of life. The aesthetic and spiritual dimensions of life can bring great fulfillment and peace.

Looking at the principle behind the specific command

- Key Concept: The balance of work and rest
- Balance of the three aspects of human life: physical, intellectual and spiritual
- Action Step: Evaluate your need to adjust your schedule and balance your life.

DIG DEEPER
Genesis 2:1-3; Ecclesiastes 3:1-15; Mark 2:27-28; Colossians 2:16-17

APPLY
What, if anything, interferes with the weekly rhythm God desires for me? What steps should I take this week that will improve my balance? What can I do on my Sabbath that will delight my heavenly Father? How can I apply this principle in my leadership style?

PRAY
"Gentle Shepherd, please lead me to delight You with a more balanced lifestyle. Teach me how you want me to spend my Sabbath."

Day 32

RESPECTING AUTHORITY AT HOME

"Honor your father and your mother, that your days may be prolonged in the land which the Lord your God gives you."
Exodus 20:12

OBSERVE
Ephesians 6:1-3

> *"Children, obey your parents in the Lord, for this is right. Honor your Father and Mother (which is the first commandment with a promise), that it may be well with you, and that you may live long on the earth."*

1 Timothy 3:1-5

> *"It is a trustworthy statement: if any man aspires to the office of overseer, it is a fine work he desires to do. An overseer, then, must be above reproach, the husband of one wife, temperate, prudent, respectable, hospitable, able to teach, not addicted to wine or pugnacious, but gentle, uncontentious, free from the love of money. He must be one who manages his own household well, keeping his children under control with all dignity (but if a man does not know how to manage his own household, how will he take care of the church of God?)"*

KEY PRINCIPLE: Leaders first lead in their family by honoring age and experience.

UNDERSTAND
The most important social unit on earth is the family. No institution in history has exerted more influence on individuals than the family. Yet, perhaps no institution today is under greater attack than the family.

This command calls us back to the ancient path of wisdom concerning our perception of, and respect for, basic family roles and responsibilities. We learn from this command that God intends a marriage to be a covenant between one and one woman. We also see from the word "honor" as used here, and by the pairing of the terms "honor" and "obey" in Ephesians 6:1-3, that God intends children to honor their parents by obeying them.

The passage quoted above from 1 Timothy indicates that one criterion for church leadership selection is that children of the prospective elder should respect and obey him.

As the years pass by, our respect for our parents continues even after we leave home and lead our own household. God wants us to be thankful for what we received and learned from our parents. He wants us to express that gratitude in ways that our parents understand and accept. This respect continues even through the tough times when adult children virtually become their parents' "parents," honoring and taking care of them until their death. This principle also extends to other senior friends whom God has used to influence us. God often brings individuals into our lives who mentor us, giving us the benefit of their insight, their experience, and their counsel. Those nourishing, encouraging people are gifts to us from God.

In the Western world we worship youth and avoid all signs of advancing adulthood. In contrast to that futile philosophy, this ancient principle exhorts us to value age and experience. This principle elevates inner wisdom over outer appearance. We can anticipate wisdom, tranquility, and continuity by obeying this commandment.

Some Bible scholars believe that the reference to long life does not focus on chronological age, but rather the quality of life that one has during their later years. The most powerful influence that a parent has on his or her children is the example they demonstrate to them. A young father who neglects or abandons his parents will probably experience that neglect by his own children. A story is told of a father who places his ailing parent in a cart and begins to take him into a wilderness. The father's young son asks where he is taking his grandparent. The father explains that the aged one is sick, non-productive and must be taken to a special place to die. The young child then asks if he can go along. The father refuses. The child demands that he must go. The father inquires why the son feels it is necessary to go along. The son replies, "So I will know where to take you, when you are old and unproductive."

DIG DEEPER
Proverbs 22:6; Jeremiah 35:1-19

APPLY
How can I honor my father and mother this week? Who else, from whose care and experience I have benefited, should I contact with an expression of thankfulness or respect? How does God want us to understand the promise that accompanies this command? How can I apply this principle in leadership?

PRAY
"Heavenly Father, please help me be the parent that my children are pleased to honor and obey. Show me the ways You want me to express honor to my parents—and others You brought into my life to teach and guide me—this week."

Day 33

RESPECTING OTHERS

"You shall love the Lord your God with all your heart, and with all your soul, and with all your mind. This is the great and foremost commandment. The second is like it, 'You shall love your neighbor as yourself.' On these two commandments depend the whole Law and the Prophets."
Matthew 22:37-40

OBSERVE
Exodus 20:13-16

> *You shall not murder.*
> *You shall not commit adultery.*
> *You shall not steal.*
> *You shall not bear false witness against your neighbor.*

KEY PRINCIPLE: Leaders demonstrate their love for others.

UNDERSTAND
With the sixth commandment, "Do not murder," God calls us to respect His marvelous creation of life. This command should be interpreted in the context of all scripture. Genesis 9:5-6, for example, endorses capital punishment. In other words, God distinguishes between murder and justifiable killing.

God wants society to protect its powerless people, young and old. Psalm 10:14 says of God, "The helpless put their trust in you. You are the defender of orphans." Proverbs 22:22-23 warns, "Do not rob the poor because they are poor or exploit the needy in court. For the LORD is their defender. He will injure anyone who injures them." If we follow His example, we too will respect and protect human life.

The seventh commandment, "Do not commit adultery," calls us to respect the sanctity of marriage and protect that commitment from violation. Faithfulness to marriage vows is a priceless gift for a husband and wife to give each other. It is also a priceless gift to the children of that family. A person's faithfulness to marriage vows is also significant to those who work with that man or woman. After all, if a person is willing to violate a marriage vow, how safe are agreements made with his or her colleagues at work?

We observe the eighth commandment, "Do not steal," by respecting the property rights of others. Our respect for this principle should extend from neighbors' tools, office supplies, and music copyrights to international respect for the assets and safety of other countries. Respect for property extends to vandalism, trespassing and "tagging."

The ninth commandment addresses the issue of integrity in what we say about others. How many lives have been turned upside down by the false statements of others, whether from malice or carelessness? Truthfulness builds respect and trustworthiness.

Looking at the principles behind the specific commands:

Commandment #6 – Respect Human Life
- Key Concept: Recognize the importance of all human life.
- No lesser status based upon race, gender, age or anything else
- Action Step: Protect those who depend on your leadership and influence

Commandment #7 – The Family
- Key Concept: Importance of family institution; sexual purity
- Commitment to family most solemn societal relationship
- Betrayal of family erodes trust in other relationships
- Action Step: Honor your family in all areas of your life.

Commandment #8 – Property Rights
- Key Concept: Respect the property of others
- Goes beyond stealing, includes trespassing, vandalism and granting privacy
- Prevents social instability and interpersonal conflict.
- Action Step: Make a personal decision not to take materials from your work or steal time from your employer.

Commandment #9 – Integrity
- Key Concept: To be honest and tell the truth
- Results in mutual trust, respect and compatibility
- Action Step: Seek to be straightforward and transparent in with others.

DIG DEEPER
Exodus 22:2; Matthew 5:21-30; Hebrews 13:4; Proverbs 6:16-20

APPLY
How well am I protecting those who depend on my influence? How am I demonstrating my commitment to my current or future marriage? Am I truthful in all my comments about others? How can I apply these principles in my leadership style?

PRAY
"Heavenly Father, please give me love for others as I acknowledge their human dignity, respect their property, walk in integrity and honor my family in every way."

Day 34

BEING THANKFUL AND CONTENT

". . . the removing of those things which can be shaken, as of created things, in order that those things which cannot be shaken may remain. Therefore, since we receive a kingdom which cannot be shaken, let us show gratitude, by which we may offer to God an acceptable service with reverence and awe."
Hebrews 12:27-29 (NLT)

OBSERVE
Exodus 20:17

> "*You shall not covet your neighbor's house; you shall not covet your neighbor's wife or his male servant or his female servant or his ox or his donkey or anything that belongs to your neighbor.*"

KEY PRINCIPLE: Leaders are thankful and content.

UNDERSTAND
At the root of many societal problems is the selfish desire, sometimes evil desire, to have what others possess. (See Matthew 15:19.) When we envy others, we disobey this command. When we resent the fact that others have what we want, we fail this test. Covetousness is at the core of corruption, a global social and economic disease.

One powerful antidote to the venom of covetousness is contentment. Covetousness says we must have what we want. Contentment replies that we will have what we want when we want what we have!

Contentment is not based on material wealth. Some very rich and very poor people are covetous, and other very rich and very poor people are content. Paul wrote: *"But I rejoiced in the Lord greatly, that*

now at last you have revived your concern for me; indeed, you were concerned before but you lacked opportunity. Not that I speak from want; for I have learned to be content in whatever circumstances I am. I know how to get along with humble means, and I also know how to live in prosperity; in any and every circumstance I have learned the secret of being filled and going hungry, both of having abundance and suffering need. I can do all things through Him who strengthens me."
Philippians 4:10-13

A key characteristic of contentment is thankfulness. To be thankful is to be thoughtful. As we think of all God has given us, and as we ponder the many ways our family and friends have encouraged and blessed us, these thoughts fill our minds and crowd out the covetous thoughts that might otherwise take root.

> *"And let the peace of Christ rule in your hearts, to which indeed you were called in one body; and be thankful. Let the word of Christ richly dwell within you, with all wisdom teaching and admonishing one another with psalms and hymns and spiritual songs, singing with thankfulness in your hearts to God. And whatever you do in word or deed, do all in the name of the Lord Jesus, giving thanks through Him to God the Father."*
> Colossians 3:15-17

It is possible to have healthy ambition without violating this principle. Setting personal goals and working toward them does not necessarily involve envy. Having ambition will not automatically rule out contentment. Living in the present and being grateful for today's reality is an indication of contentment. Being consumed with the future to the neglect of the present is one of the indications of ignoring this principle. Set goals, prepare for the future; but enjoy the "now" and be grateful for what you have. This results in happiness – a very important condition that eludes many in our materialistic society.

Looking at the principle behind the specific command

Commandment #10 – Contentment
- Key Concept: Learn to be contented with what you have.
- Contentment is a state of mind.
- It is possible to have much and not be contented; it is possible to be poor and be contented.
- Action Step: Develop a grateful spirit.

DIG DEEPER
Romans 7:7-9; 2 Corinthians 12:10; Ephesians 5:18-20; Colossians 3:1-5; 1 Timothy 6:8

APPLY
Who do I envy, and why? Who, or what, am I thankful for today? How can I apply this principle to my leadership?

PRAY
"Father, the enemy would consume me with covetousness. I pray today that Your Holy Spirit will consume me with contentment and thankfulness. Please help me do this not only for my benefit, but also—and even more so—for Your glory."

Day 35

DOERS OF THE WORD

"Oh, that they would always have hearts like this, that they might fear me and obey all my commands! If they did, they and their descendants would prosper forever."
Deuteronomy 5:29

Looking back over the week, I learned . . .

Day 29 - Leaders earn respect by showing respect.

Day 30 - Leaders are loyal to the authority of Almighty God.

Day 31 - Leaders honor God when they follow His example of Sabbath rest.

Day 32 - Leaders first lead in their family.

Day 33 - Leaders love others.

Day 34 - Leaders are thankful and content.

Journal Space

Lord, I am grateful for you teaching me the following:

Lord, I plan on being a leader who follows God by:

I have questions about:

Day 36

REACHING EXCELLENCE IN LEADERSHIP INVOLVES GOD'S HELP

". . . but our adequacy is from God"
2 Corinthians 3:5

OBSERVE
2 Corinthians 3:1-5

> *"Are we beginning to commend ourselves again? Or do we need, as some, letters of commendation to you or from you? You are our letter, written in our hearts, known and read by all men; being manifested that you are a letter of Christ, cared for by us, written not with ink, but with the Spirit of the living God, not on tablets of stone, but on tablets of human hearts. And such confidence we have through Christ toward God. Not that we are adequate in ourselves to consider anything as coming from ourselves, but our adequacy is from God."*

KEY PRINCIPLE: God can make you adequate to achieve excellence in leadership.

UNDERSTAND
In this passage the Apostle Paul is describing his credentials as a leader who actually led his followers in a life changing process. He explains that he does not need letters of reference or commendation about his ability to lead. He states that they (the Corinthians) are living testimony to his effectiveness as a leader. He points out the fact that their changed lives are "letters . . . know and read by all men." In other words, the amazing positive change in the behavior and attitudes of the Corinthians (infamous in the ancient world as depraved and decadent) gave mute evidence of his leadership ability.

Paul, in his leadership, had penetrated through their behavior and thinking to their very hearts. He stated that they were letters not written with ink, "but with the Spirit of the living God, not on tablets of stone, but on tablets of human hearts." In this amazing statement, Paul gives the credit for his life changing leadership ability to God. He makes it clear that life changing leadership requires the power of God in the leader's life.

Leading with the character traits we have examined in this study is very difficult to accomplish. In today's devotional study, Paul has written about his secret for achieving the difficult status of being an effective leader. He depended upon and received God's help.

At the conclusion of the Pointman Leadership Institute seminars, many of the participants indicate that they are willing to accept the eight character traits that are presented as valid requirements of powerful leadership. But many often remark that these character traits are difficult to achieve. They are not difficult. They are impossible to achieve without God's help.

This week, we will focus on how to obtain the help of God in your life.

DIG DEEPER
Philippians 4:13; Exodus 3:11-12; Isaiah 41:10; 2 Thessalonians 2:15-17

APPLY
Do I draw upon the power and wisdom that God gives, or do I rely on my own determination, intellect and charisma?

PRAY
"Lord, help me to understand the mighty power that is available to me through you; and then turn to you for this power."

Day 37

WE ARE ESTRANGED FROM GOD IN OUR NATURAL STATE

"But a natural man does not accept the things of the Spirit of God"
1 Corinthians 2:14

OBSERVE
1 Corinthians 2:10-15

> *"For to us God revealed them through the Spirit; for the Spirit searches all things, even the depths of God. For who among men knows the thoughts of a man except the spirit of the man, which is in him? Even so the thoughts of God no one knows except the Spirit of God. Now we have received, not the spirit of the world, but the Spirit who is from God, that we might know the things freely given to us by God, which things we also speak, not in words taught by human wisdom, but in those taught by the Spirit, combining spiritual thoughts with spiritual words. But a natural man does not accept the things of the Spirit of God; for they are foolishness to him, and he cannot understand them, because they are spiritually appraised."*

Romans 3:23

> *"For all have sinned and fall short of the glory of God."*

Romans 5: 12

> *"Therefore, just as through one man sin entered the world, and death through sin, and so death (spiritual) spread to all men..."*

KEY PRINCIPLE: We must have God's Holy Spirit within us in order to receive and understand His wisdom.

UNDERSTAND

In these passages from the Bible we can see that every human being in his or her natural state cannot understand the wisdom of God, or have contact with Him because we have inherited spiritual death. We are a born with a body that has an eternal soul, but a dead spirit. God offers His Holy Spirit to replace the void of our dead spirit that is the result of sin.

In the first passage, Paul is talking to new followers of Jesus who have recently received the Holy Spirit of God. This Holy Spirit has given them the ability to understand the wisdom of God and also receive the adequacy that God freely gives to those who have His spirit (*"that we might know the things freely given to us by God"*) These new followers had transitioned from their natural state to the state of being spiritually alive. In order to make this transition, one must first recognize their current state of spiritual death.

There is much confusion about how God classifies someone as a "sinner." Some think that it is a relative classification. They believe that God grades on "the curve." In other words, if one is better than average in his or her behavior, he or she will not be classified as a sinner. In Romans 3:23, God makes his definition clear. He states: *"For all have sinned and fall short of the glory of God."* The phrase "fall short of the glory of God," makes the definition easy to understand. If one is not equal with God (He is perfect and holy) then he or she is a sinner. That definition includes all humans.

The passage from Romans 5:12, explains that we sin because we are sinners; we are not sinners because we sin. In other words, we are all born sinners and therefore do not have a natural connection with God. On the contrary we cannot know Him or draw upon his wisdom and help in our natural state.

DIG DEEPER
Ephesians 2:1-5; 1 Corinthian 6:8-11; 1 Corinthians 15:20-22

APPLY
Have I admitted to myself and God that in my natural state, I do not have a relationship with God, which makes his wisdom and help unavailable?

PRAY
"Lord, help me to understand the significance of having a personal relationship with you through your son Jesus Christ."

Day 38

JESUS CHRIST CAME TO RECONCILE US TO GOD

"For if while we were enemies, we were reconciled to God through the death of His Son, much more, having been reconciled, we shall be saved by His life."
Romans 5:10

OBSERVE
Romans 5:6-11

> *"For while we were still helpless, at the right time Christ died for the ungodly. For one will hardly die for a righteous man; though perhaps for the good man someone would dare even to die. But God demonstrates His own love toward us, in that while we were yet sinners, Christ died for us. Much more then, having now been justified by His blood, we shall be saved from the wrath of God through Him. For if while we were enemies, we were reconciled to God through the death of His Son, much more, having been reconciled, we shall be saved by His life. And not only this, but we also exult in God through our Lord Jesus Christ, through whom we have now received the reconciliation."*

John 3:16-19

> *"For God so loved the world, that He gave His only begotten Son, that whoever believes in Him should not perish, but have eternal life. For God did not send the Son into the world to judge the world, but that the world should be saved through Him. He who believes in Him is not judged; he who does not believe has been judged already, because he has not believed in the name of the only begotten Son of God. And this is the*

judgment, that light is come into the world, and men loved the darkness rather than the light; for their deeds were evil."

KEY PRINCIPLE: The way to obtain spiritual life is through Jesus Christ.

UNDERSTAND

We have learned that in our natural state we are estranged from God and do not have spiritual life. In today's passages we learn that God provided a means for reconciliation. He sent his only begotten son Jesus Christ to earth. Jesus is God's communication ("Word" from John 1) of love and reconciliation.

Jesus was born miraculously without a human father. The Bible states that: "When His mother Mary had been betrothed to Joseph, before they came together, she was found to be with child by the Holy Spirit." (Matthew 1: 18)

He lived a perfect life and voluntarily suffered a horrible death by crucifixion. He was resurrected from the dead and lives today at the right hand of God the Father in heaven (Hebrews 1:3).

The purpose of His life, death and resurrection was to purchase our redemption and make it possible for our reconciliation with God. When we place our faith in His plan and receive Him as our Savior from sin, our reconciliation is complete and we are made alive spiritually. From that point on, we have a personal relationship with God through the Holy Spirit who indwells us. This is why Jesus said to the Jewish nobleman Nicodemus that he must be born again (John 3:4). Jesus was talking about a spiritual rebirth.

Jesus said: *". . . he who hears My word, and believes Him who sent Me, has eternal life, and does not come into judgment, but has passed out of death (spiritual) into life."* (John 5:24)

DIG DEEPER
1 Peter 1:18-21; 2 Corinthians 5:17-21

APPLY
Have I recognized Jesus Christ as God's only provision for spiritual life?

PRAY
"Lord, give me the humility acknowledge Jesus Christ as your Son and the only way to be reconciled to you."

Day 39

THE SIGNIFICANCE OF CONFESSION

"If we confess our sins, He is faithful and righteous to forgive us our sins and to cleanse us from all unrighteousness."
1 John 1:9

OBSERVE
1 John 1:5-10

> *"And this is the message we have heard from Him and announce to you, that God is light, and in Him there is no darkness at all. If we say that we have fellowship with Him and yet walk in the darkness, we lie and do not practice the truth; but if we walk in the light as He Himself is in the light, we have fellowship with one another, and the blood of Jesus His Son cleanses us from all sin. If we say that we have no sin, we are deceiving ourselves, and the truth is not in us. If we confess our sins, He is faithful and righteous to forgive us our sins and to cleanse us from all unrighteousness. If we say that we have not sinned, we make Him a liar, and His word is not in us."*

KEY PRINCIPLE: Confession is a necessary step in God's reconciliation process.

UNDERSTAND
Confession is a word familiar to those in the criminal justice system. Literally, it means to agree with a charge made against you. For example, if a police officer confronts a suspected criminal with evidence connecting him or her to a crime and the suspect admits his or her involvement--that is a confession. If confession means agreeing with a charge made against one, then what is the charge God has made against us? Reading the above passage make the answer clear. We must agree with God that we are guilty of sinning.

This passage was written to believers. We learn from reading it that genuine followers of Jesus agree with God about being sinners. The tense of the word "confession" indicates a continual process. We begin our relationship with God by agreeing with Him about our sinful nature. We grow in that relationship by continuing to confess our dependence upon Him confessing specific sins as necessary. This passage explains that confession is characteristic of true believers. It is a threshold issue.

In His first sermon ("Sermon on the Mount") Jesus begins by saying: "Blessed are the poor in spirit, for theirs is the kingdom of heaven (Matthew 5:3). In other words, Jesus taught us that the first step in seeing the "kingdom of heaven" involves declaring spiritual bankruptcy or confessing one's status as a helpless sinner. This is the opposite of self sufficiency. To some, this is a very difficult step to take. It is in our nature to want to do things ourselves. Confessing that we are "sinners" and that we cannot "fix" this deficiency on our own goes against that nature. First, we don't like to be "wrong." Secondly, we don't like to admit that we are unable to correct our situation alone. But this must be done. It is humbling; but necessary. Our nature tells us we can earn God's acceptance. We want to find our own way. We can somehow make it on our own. But the Bible is clear on this issue. We must be willing to admit we "fall short of God's glory" (Romans 3:23); and therefore are sinners in God's sight, with our only hope being in Jesus the Savior.

King David was guilty of adultery and then murdered to cover up his sin. Yet, God placed him in a significant position of leadership and used him significantly even after his sin--because David was willing to confess (see Psalms 32).

DIG DEEPER
Psalms 32; James 5:16; Proverbs 28:13

APPLY

Have I confessed my sinful nature to God, agreeing with Him that I am a sinner?

PRAY

"Lord, I admit that I am a sinner. I cannot earn your blessing or acceptance. I am sorry for my sin. I agree with you that Jesus is my only hope for salvation."

Day 40

REPENTANCE BRINGS US TO A POSITION WHERE WE CAN BE STRENGTHENED BY GOD

"For the sorrow that is according to the will of God produces a repentance without regret, leading to salvation."
2 Corinthians 7:10

OBSERVE
2 Corinthians 7:8-10

> *"For though I caused you sorrow by my letter, I do not regret it; though I did regret it--for I see that that letter caused you sorrow, though only for a while--I now rejoice, not that you were made sorrowful, but that you were made sorrowful to the point of **repentance**; for you were made sorrowful according to the will of God, in order that you might not suffer loss in anything through us. For the sorrow that is according to the will of God produces a **repentance** without regret, leading to salvation; but the sorrow of the world produces death."*

KEY PRINCIPLE: Repentance means turning to God from our own sinful way.

UNDERSTAND
When most people come to an understanding that we are all sinners in God's eyes, they are sorry for their sins. This is a good reaction. In the above passage of scripture we learn that one can be sorry without repenting. The Bible is clear about the importance of going beyond being sorrowful and actually repenting.

In Isaiah 53:6, (circa 750 BC) the Bible explains that the reason God would place our sin on the coming Messiah is that we have all turned to his or her own way. The word repentance means an "about face" or a **turning** from one direction to another. In the Bible we see this concept being important in establishing a relationship with God. It is used almost interchangeably with being born again or becoming a follower of Jesus. For example in Mark 1:15, Jesus urges men to "**repent** and believe in the Gospel." In Luke 24:47 Jesus announces that "**repentance** for forgiveness of sins should be proclaimed in His name to all the nations. . . "

Many people come to God in times of need and ask Him to help them. They even indicate their belief in Him. Asking for God to join us and bless us as we go our own way **is not repentance**. Repentance is being willing to turn from our way to God. Repentance is not an act that earns us God's favor. It is a willingness to submit to Him and ask Him to make us into the person He wants us to be--to go His way. We do not have the ability to go God's way without Him in our life. He has the power to begin changing our lives as we turn to Him from our own way.

The Bible clearly states that our salvation is a gift from God that we cannot earn. Therefore, repentance does not mean we must change our lifestyle until we are acceptable by God. Rather it means we admit to God that we cannot change in our own strength, and are **turning** from our own way to Him for the strength **only He can provide**. True repentance is followed by a commitment to discover all one can about "God's way," as we depend upon His strength to live it.

DIG DEEPER
Isaiah 53:1-9; Acts 26:18-20; Acts 11:18; Acts 17:30

APPLY
Have I been willing to turn from my own way to God? Have I been willing to surrender to His way in my life?

PRAY

"Lord, I am willing to turn from my own way to you. I do not have the strength to live as you want me to live. I am turning in surrender to you, asking you to help me to reach the plan you have for my life."

Day 41

TAKING SIMPLE BELIEF TO THE POINT OF TRUSTING FAITH

"But without faith it is impossible to please Him."
Hebrews 11:6

OBSERVE
Hebrews 11:1-6

> *"Now faith is the assurance of things hoped for, the conviction of things not seen. For by it the men of old gained approval. By* **faith** *we understand that the worlds were prepared by the word of God, so that what is seen was not made out of things which are visible. By faith Abel offered to God a better sacrifice than Cain, through which he obtained the testimony that he was righteous, God testifying about his gifts, and through faith, though he is dead, he still speaks. By faith Enoch was taken up so that he should not see death; and he was not found because God took him up; for he obtained the witness that before his being taken up he was pleasing to God. And without* **faith** *it is impossible to please Him, for he who comes to God must believe that He is, and that He is a rewarder of those who seek Him."*

KEY PRINCIPLE: Faith is the key factor in establishing a relationship with God.

UNDERSTAND
This passage from the Bible tells us that without faith, we cannot please God. Faith is all important. Yet there seems to be confusion about the implications of "faith." In the Bible we read: *"You believe that God is one. You do well; the demons also believe, and shudder."*

(James 2:19) This passage seems to indicate that simple belief is not enough.

Surveys continue to reveal that a majority of people in the world believe in God or a supreme being. In the United States a strong majority believe in Jesus Christ. However, simple intellectual assent to a fact does not necessarily mean one has faith in that fact. There is a difference between simple belief and life changing faith. Belief can be impersonal and just an intellectual exercise. Faith involves a strong belief that results in personal trust.

Two police officers were shot in separate incidents just two weeks apart. They were both shot in the chest. One died within seconds. The other survived. These similar incidents had one significant difference. One officer was wearing a ballistic vest (bullet proof armor). Both officers owned the armor. Both believed in the armor. One took his belief to the point of commitment--he wore the vest. The other chose not to wear his vest. The point is that belief in the vest is not enough. The vest can only protect an officer if he chooses to place his faith in the vest by wearing it.

In the Bible we read the following about faith: "For by grace you have been saved through **faith**; and that not of yourselves, it is the gift of God" (Ephesians 2:8)

DIG DEEPER
Ephesians 2:1-10; John 1:12; 1 John 5:11,12

APPLY
Have I taken my belief in Jesus Christ to the point of commitment? Have I "received" Jesus Christ as my personal Savior?

PRAY

"Lord, I not only believe in you; I desire to place my faith upon you. I want you to come into my life and make me the person you want me to be."

Day 42

DOERS OF THE WORD

"But prove yourselves doers of the word, and not merely hearers who delude themselves. For if anyone is a hearer of the word and not a doer, he is like a man who looks at his natural face in a mirror; for once he has looked at himself and gone away, he has immediately forgotten what kind of person he was. But one who looks intently at the perfect law, the law of liberty, and abides by it, not having become a forgetful hearer but an effectual doer, this man shall be blessed in what he does."
James 1:22-25

Looking back over the week, I learned . . .

Day 36 - Excellence in leadership requires God's help.

Day 37 - Our natural state--estranged from God.

Day 38 - Reconciled by Jesus Christ.

Day 39 - The significance of confession.

Day 40 - The significance of repentance.

Day 41 - The difference between belief and faith.

If you have taken your faith to the point of repentance and commitment and prayed yesterday's prayer sincerely, then you have been born again. You are alive spiritually. Now, you need to follow the exhortation of Jesus to publicly declare (confess) Him as your Lord. *"Everyone therefore who shall confess Me before men, I will also confess him before My Father who is in heaven."* (Matthew 10:32). A decision to establish a personal relationship with God through His son Jesus Christ is a very significant decision that has eternal implications. You have been "born again." But now there is life after birth.

Journal Space

Lord, I am grateful for you teaching me the following:

Lord, I plan on being a doer of the Word by:

I have questions about:

Conclusions

This Six Week Daily Devotional is intended to support people who are interested in discovering the principles of leadership that God identifies and illustrates in His Word or message to us (The Bible). It is also intended to stimulate an interest in the spiritual dimension of life.

The following is a three point-prayer that has helped many to begin their relationship with God through Jesus Christ.

(1) The Prayer of Confession: This first step means admitting to God that you are not perfect like Him; and therefore are a sinner. The Bible states: *"For all have sinned and fall short of the glory of God"* (Romans 3:23). The phrase "fall short" explains how God classifies sinners. All who fall short of His perfection are "sinners."

(2) The Prayer of Repentance: Repentance means a change of direction. Jesus spoke often of the necessity of this action. This prayer is centered on our willingness to turn from "our own way" to the Lord, who alone is able to make us into the people He wants us to be. The Bible says we must turn to God and seek His help in being the person He wants us to be (Acts 26:20). Many people who believe in the Lord have not repented. Many do ask for God's help when they experience difficulties, but they do not "turn" to Him. Rather, they ask the Lord to come join them as they continue going their own way.

(3) The Prayer of Commitment: There is a difference between belief and trust. The Bible says: *"He came unto His own creation; but His own received Him not. But as many as received Him, to them He gave the power to become the sons of God."* (John 1:12). This prayer is taking one's belief in the Lord to the point of commitment. It means inviting the Lord Jesus to come into your life.

"And you will seek Me and find Me, when you search for Me with all your heart." Jeremiah 29:13